TEXAS PEOPLE, TEXAS PLACES

For Kathy and Okey,
with best wishes
Lonn Taylor

TEXAS PEOPLE, TEXAS PLACES

MORE MUSINGS OF THE <u>RAMBLING BOY</u>

LONN TAYLOR

Foreword by
Joe Nick Patoski

Linoleum cuts by
Barbara Mathews Whitehead

Fort Worth, Texas

Library of Congress Cataloging-in-Publication Data

Taylor, Lonn, 1940- author.
Texas people, Texas places : more musings of the Rambling Boy / Lonn Taylor.
    pages cm
The Rambling Boy was a newspaper column with Lonn Taylor's stories about
the people and places of Texas.
ISBN 978-0-87565-581-9 (alk. paper)
1. Texas–Social life and customs–Anecdotes. 2. Texas–Biography–Anecdotes.
3. Texas–Description and travel–Anecdotes. 4. Texas–History, Local–
Anecdotes. 5. Characters and characteristics–Texas–Anecdotes. 6. Cities and
towns–Texas–Anecdotes. 7. Taylor, Lonn, 1940—Childhood and youth–
Anecdotes. I. Title.
F386.6.T39 2014
976.4–dc23
                              2013042132

TCU Press
TCU Box 298300
Fort Worth, Texas 76129
817.257.7822
www.prs.tcu.edu
To order books: 1.800.826.8911

✛

designed & illustrated by
Barbara Mathews Whitehead

✛

For Dedie,
Best loved

CONTENTS

II. TEXAS PLACES

FOREWORD

IN FAR WEST TEXAS, where Lonn Taylor lives, there's a saying that if you ask someone a question, they'll tell you a story. And out there, no one tells stories quite like Lonn. That's no brag, just fact.

It's taken me some years and considerable miles to reach that conclusion. I knew Lonn was a fellow traveler from my hometown of Fort Worth long ago. I didn't know that his family was actually from McKinney and that he'd spent much of his youth in the Philippines, where his father built roads.

His twenty-year career as curator and historian at the Smithsonian Institution in Washington, DC, attests to his vast reservoir of knowledge and love of history. Less well known is his insightful understanding of the kind of Texas history that textbooks and museums tend to overlook. That belated discovery began with his innocent question, asked in a rich, distinctive voice inflected with a slight drawl that makes clear he could come from nowhere else but Texas: "Do you know Pepi Plowman?"

She's my friend, my wife and I told him excitedly, a renaissance artist who happened to be Janis Joplin's roommate in the ghetto apartments near the University of Texas, the same scene that produced underground cartoonist Gilbert Shelton and musician Powell St. John and ultimately germinated into Austin's global reputation as the creative city it is today.

Lonn already knew all that because he was there, it turns out, and saw it all.

Lonn is especially well versed in all things Texas. "He can stand anywhere in Texas and tell you the history of each parcel of land on either side of the road and the role it played in the development of Texas, going all the way back to the days of the

Republic," marveled Eddie Wilson, the trail boss of the Armadillo World Headquarters, Austin's most storied music venue.

Wilson recalled running into Lonn at a Fort Worth pizza parlor and at a bar in Austin during the mid sixties. Both times, Lonn was with a group of gentlemen wearing tweed who were hanging on to every word Lonn spoke. Turns out they were neither academics nor the historian types Lonn runs with; they were a rock and roll band called the Sir Douglas Quintet, a Texas group that had embraced British couture, as had Lonn, who fancied a bowler hat.

This was about the same time that Lonn was scouting for period furniture to furnish the interiors of the University of Texas's Winedale Historical Center, a historic site between LaGrange and Brenham. Then again, he was working on a book about early Texas furniture, collaborating with no less than Miss Ima Hogg, a Texas icon if there ever was one, so he knew what to look for. He was also the director and curator of Winedale. In other words, he wore many hats, not just bowlers.

There have been other stops along the way, including Dallas and Santa Fe. But it wasn't until 2002, after he retired from the Smithsonian, and his lovely wife Edith (Dedie) retired as a senior editor of the *Chronicle of Higher Education*, and the couple relocated to Fort Davis, Texas's mountain village in the western end of the state, that Lonn Taylor really found his voice.

The *Rambling Boy* started appearing in the *Desert-Mountain Times* in 2003 until that publication folded, and has run ever since in the *Big Bend Sentinel* of Marfa. Every week, his stories about the people and places of Texas are featured in the finest weekly newspaper in the state, and he then reads them aloud in his sonorous drawl on Marfa's public radio station, KRTS.

After tramping all over God's green and brown earth, he's more at home than ever, and more in love with Texas than anyone I know. Lonn writes it, talks it, walks it, sings it, lives it, and breathes it. Dobie, Bedichek, and Webb—eat your hearts out.

In a recent *Rambling Boy* column, ninety-three-year-old Hope Wilson told Lonn all about the rise and fall of the Pecos cantaloupe, the sweetest, creamiest melon ever grown. She prefaced her remarks by telling him, "You may write down anything I say. I did not go to the school of lies and promises."

Neither did Lonn, who has a way of pulling statements like that out of good people who might not otherwise be prone to share their wisdom.

Like I said, no brag, just facts, all of them writ large.

Joe Nick Patoski
Wimberly, Texas
August 2012

INTRODUCTION

I HAVE ALWAYS BEEN attracted to eccentric people and small towns. In high school my best friends were not the athletes or the beauty queens but the shy girls who wanted to be artists and the quiet boys who played chess. As an undergraduate, even though I majored in history and government, I hung around with theater majors and ballet dancers and would-be beatniks. As a young man I came very close to marrying a budding actress, until one day in her company I idly remarked that I wished I could play the piano, and she said, "Why would you want to play the piano? I don't have a piano," and I suddenly realized that her most powerful driving force was not libido, as I had thought, but ego. I have spent countless hours listening to oddballs tell me their life stories in bars, cafés, bus stations, and on the porches of country stores, and for the most part they have been rewarding hours. I used to have an empty billfold that an old man named Dick Proctor, a carnival cook, gave me after I picked him up hitchhiking just north of Austin. He was going to Waco to rejoin his carnival, having gotten drunk and been left behind in Austin, and he entertained me all the way to Waco with stories about his life on the rodeo circuit. When I let him out of the car at the carnival grounds, he reached into his pocket, pulled out his battered wallet, emptied it of the few bills that were in it, wrote something in pencil on a slip of paper from a notebook in his shirt pocket, inserted the paper in the wallet, and handed it to me, saying, "Here, I'd like you to have something to remember me by." When I looked in the wallet I saw that he had written on the paper, "Dick Proctor, World's Champion Cowboy, 1928." I have never checked to see if he had really held that title, or wondered how many of his stories were true. They were all good stories.

When I was a teenager I got hold of a book by Joseph Mitchell called *McSorley's Wonderful Saloon,* a collection of pieces about eccentric New Yorkers that Mitchell had published in the *New Yorker* in the 1930s. That book became a talisman for me, and I decided that when I became a writer I would try to write about the kinds of people Mitchell wrote about. When I moved to New York to go to graduate school, I tracked down McSorley's, a scruffy place on Seventh Street near the Bowery that had a sign in the window that said, "Good Ale, Raw Onions, No Ladies," and I spent several evenings there, but the characters that Mitchell had written about were long gone. It was not until I returned to Texas that I realized that Texas was full of places like McSorley's. Many of them were in small towns—places like Joe Matejewski's store in Nechanitz or Olympia's Saloon in Mingus—where you could meet all of the eccentrics that you wanted any afternoon and listen to tall tales until closing time. Some of them were in urban settings. I once saw a man with a stepladder and half a dozen little dogs come into Bonnies Only Barbecue on Fifth Street in Austin and proceed to put the dogs through their paces on the stepladder. He explained that he had a trained dog act that he took to rodeos, and his wife would not let the dogs practice at home. Joseph Mitchell would have loved him.

I cannot explain my desire to listen to and record people who live on the periphery of society; it is just part of who I am. Nor can I explain my attraction to small towns. I was not a small-town boy. My childhood was divided between Fort Worth, Texas, which is no Podunk, and Manila, Philippines, which, when my family lived there, was the most cosmopolitan city in Southeast Asia. I have lived in New York, Santa Fe, and Washington, DC, and have savored the metropolitan delights of those cities. But I also spent seven years running a historic site in Round Top, Texas, population seventy, and now I live in Fort Davis, Texas, which has 1,160 people but no traffic lights and few paved streets.

I enjoy the intimacy and informality of small-town life, the fact that everyone you see has time to stop and talk, the fact that after you have lived in a small town for a while you become a member of an extended family, even though unless you were born there you will always be a peripheral member. In Round Top, if you did not show up at the post office to pick up your mail for two days in a row, someone would call your house and ask, "You-all all right out there?" It was not just idle curiosity. People in small towns care about each other.

I learned to drive in the mid-1950s by making forays in my parents' big DeSoto sedan from Fort Worth to outlying communities like Granbury, Weatherford, and Glen Rose, and I always wanted to linger there and find out who lived in the old Victorian houses and who shopped in the stores on the town squares that sold bib overalls and hand-cranked ice cream freezers. Those towns had a magnetic pull for me.

My grandmother Taylor, who lived with us while I was growing up, had brothers and sisters and nieces and nephews who lived in a small town in Wharton County, Texas, called Hungerford, which had a population of about two hundred. Virtually all of the white people, and some of the blacks, were related to my grandmother. Some of our relatives' ancestors had settled there when Texas was still part of Mexico; others had arrived after the Civil War. They had intermarried until the families in Hungerford and the surrounding countryside were what my great-uncle Will Border called "inextricably intertwingled"; he liked to say that it was remarkable that babies born there had the normal numbers of fingers and toes.

In the 1950s Hungerford had two cotton gins, a post office, a café, and a general store, but it was the nearest thing that I had to an ancestral home, and I loved visiting there. There was something about Hungerford that involved cousins being in and out of each others' houses all day long, and never knowing ahead of time how many people were going to sit down at the table at meals, but knowing that you were related to all of them, that I found enormously comforting and that was completely missing from our suburban Fort Worth home, where I was the only child. I think that I have been viscerally attracted to small towns all my life, perhaps by genes inherited from what my grandmother called "the Hungerford bunch."

I am not a Texas exceptionalist. I am sure that there are eccentrics and interesting small towns in other states. I know from personal experience that there are in Virginia, New Mexico, and Oregon. My wife grew up in Astoria, Oregon, and her stories about fishermen and lumberjacks and Finnish communists and their hometowns can match anything heard in Texas. Once I was reading her hometown newspaper, the *Daily Astorian*, and I came across an obituary for an old gentleman who was described in the subhead as "theoretical anarchist." I asked her about him and she said, "Oh, he was just an old communist from Brownsmead." He would definitely have been worth a chapter in *McSorley's Wonderful Saloon*. But I am a Texan and I live in Texas, so Texas towns and Texas people are what I write about.

The short pieces in this book, which I think of as entertainments—they are not profound enough to be called essays—are about people and places in Texas. They all originally appeared, some in a shortened form, in the *Rambling Boy* column that I have written for nearly ten years, first for the Alpine *Desert-Mountain Times* and more recently for the Marfa *Big Bend Sentinel*. I am grateful to the publishers of both papers, Kay Taylor Burnett of Alpine and Robert and Rosario Halpern of Marfa, for permitting them to appear again.

Lonn Taylor
Fort Davis, Texas

I. TEXAS PEOPLE

✧ 1 ✧

TRAVELS WITH MY FATHER

I CANNOT GO on a long road trip without thinking about my father. He was a highway engineer, a member of the first civil engineering class to graduate from Texas A&M that studied highway construction rather than railroad construction. That was in 1924. He went on to have a long career with the US Bureau of Public Roads. He was one of the architects of the Interstate Highway System, and he retired as a regional administrator of the Federal Highway Authority, with responsibility for all federally-funded highway construction in the states of Texas, Oklahoma, Arkansas, and Louisiana.

My father was never comfortable in an office. He was happiest out on the road, looking at highway jobs. He frequently took me with him. Our drives together were our father-and-son time, and I learned a lot from them. Dad looked at the terrain with the eye of an engineer, and he tried to teach me to observe the things that he thought were important and to draw conclusions from them. When I was a child he showed me how to watch for the next water tower as we drove across West Texas together. He explained that West Texas towns large enough to have water towers were thirty miles apart, because West Texas counties were thirty miles square and the law required that the county seat be in the center of the county.

Once during a drive from Fort Worth to College Station, we drove over a rough place in the pavement, almost a trench, just north of Hillsboro. Dad slowed the car to a stop, backed up, and pulled over on the shoulder next to the deteriorating pavement. A fence line stretched away across the fields on both sides of the road. "You see what happened here?" he asked, pointing along the fence. "When they built this highway the right-of-way went right through this fence, and the contractor failed to fill the post holes properly after he took the fence down. Water got into them, the base failed, and now the pavement is failing." The lesson here was that not doing small things right at the start of a task will eventually cause big problems.

The area around Hillsboro was replete with landmarks for Dad, as he had been the federal inspector when US Highway 81 was paved through there in the late 1920s. He would always point out the first highway overpass in Texas, an iron truss bridge that had been moved from a defunct railroad to carry a county road over the highway just south of Alvarado. South of Hillsboro was a big white farmhouse that always prompted a story about a man who had been appointed to a responsible position in the Texas Highway Department during one of the Miriam Ferguson admin- istrations, which were notable for political cronyism. When the man went to start his new job, Gibb Gilchrist, the state highway engineer, politely questioned him about his qualifications. "Well, sir," the man said, "do you know that big white house west of the road four miles south of Hillsboro?" Gilchrist said that he did, and the man said, "Well, I live there." Gilchrist said he didn't see what that had to do with his qualifications for an engineering job, and the man said, "Why, when you all built that highway from Hillsboro to Waco I went down to my fence every day and watched you. I know all about how to do it."

Dad told me stories about nearly every small town in West Texas, because he had built highways through most of them. Monahans was where, when Noah got forty days and forty nights of rain, half an inch fell. Post was where a café waitress once told Dad that of course the oysters on the menu were fresh; they came down every morning on the bus from Lubbock, didn't they? Sierra

Blanca was where the sheriff once mistook Dad's black government car for a similar one being driven across Texas by Clyde Barrow and Bonnie Parker, with near-fatal results. He used to say that he married my mother because he built the paved road to Nocona and she was at the end of it.

My father was born into the horseless carriage era, and he developed a profound respect for the lethal power of the modern automobile. His interest in highway design focused on ways of ameliorating that power. Tight curves and short sight distances are dangerous, but engineers often favor them since more generous curves and longer sight distances require more right-of-way and more earth moving. Dad was quick to point out the implications of this parsimonious approach, especially when we were driving across states outside of his region. He also disliked what he called "unnecessary signage." Too many signs, he said, distracted motorists and constituted obstacles that they might hit if they lost control of their cars. He was especially contemptuous of signs telling you that you were entering or leaving a particular watershed or national forest district. "Who cares?" he would say. The one type of sign that he thought was absolutely necessary were confirming signs, the signs that tell you that you are still on the right route when you are following a highway through a city and that are so often not there after the route has made a turn. Every time I drive through a city I can hear my father muttering, "No confirming signs. What's wrong with these people?"

One of my father's minor achievements was the development of breakaway highway signs and their use on interstate highways. When I was twenty-two I lost control of my car on the Dallas-Fort Worth toll road and hit a highway sign, spending several months in the hospital with a broken femur as a result. Dad had heard that someone was working on the development of signs that had a joint in their stanchions that would cause them to collapse if struck by a car. He went to the Texas Transportation Institute at Texas A&M

and talked them into making the development of these signs their top priority, and when a workable model had been produced, he persuaded the Federal Highway Authority to adopt it as the standard sign on all interstate highways. He was prouder of those signs than he was of his role in designing the original Interstate Highway System.

My father died nineteen years ago, at the age of eighty-nine. But he is beside me every time I get behind the wheel of a car.

February 23, 2012

✤ 2 ✤

UNCLE KIT THE DRIFTER

THERE IS A sentimental ballad from the 1870s called "The Little Rosewood Casket," about a dying woman who wants a package of old love letters read to her. The chorus goes: *In a little rosewood casket / Sitting on a marble stand / There's a packet of old letters / Written by a cherished hand.* I opened a packet of old letters the other day. They were not in a rosewood casket and they are not love letters, although they are affectionate. They were written seventy years ago to my father by his uncle Christopher Columbus (Kit) Taylor and they tell a Texas story that will never find its way into a history book.

My father's Uncle Kit was the black sheep of the family. He was born in 1867 in Farmersville, Texas. When he was eighteen, while on a drunken spree, he killed a man by firing a shotgun into his house. The man was black; Uncle Kit came from a respected family. The jury sentenced him to five years in the penitentiary, but the judge gave him his choice of serving his sentence or joining the army. Uncle Kit chose the army and did not see his family again for eighteen years. He came home briefly in 1903 and stayed long enough to witness my father's birth and enter his name in the family Bible. According to my grandmother, Uncle Kit had prepared his mother for that visit with a telegram. She drove a buggy to the railroad station to meet him but did not recognize him when he got off the train. He walked up to the buggy and asked if she would give him a ride to the hotel downtown. Still not recognizing him, and thinking that her son had missed the train she told him yes and started toward the hotel. As they passed the family home he said, "Mama, why don't we stop here?" and she burst into tears. As a child I thought that was a funny story, a joke well played. Now I see the sadness in it.

Uncle Kit disappeared again and did not surface until 1940, when one of his sisters died and left her estate to be divided equally among her siblings and their heirs. The rest of the family wanted to leave Uncle Kit out, but my father, motivated as much by curiosity as a sense of justice, decided to track him down and see that he got his share. Dad found him in Southton, Texas, a flyspeck town southeast of San Antonio, where he had a job as a watchman at a small oil refinery. By then he was in his early seventies, an old man living in a shack. The letters that I opened are the letters that he wrote to my father over the next two years, telling, or more accurately, revealing, the story of his life.

They are the letters of a well-read man. He quotes Byron, Henry Grady, and Robert Burns, and in one says that his favorite poet is Thomas Campbell, a nineteenth-century Scots poet popular with elocution teachers. In a letter to the Texas Department of Public Welfare, enclosed in one of his letters to my father, he quotes lines from the poet Owen Meredith while complaining about the late arrival of his old age assistance check. The packet includes a ten-page article about the New Deal that he submitted to some newspaper, headed "Submitted at Your Usual Rate," tracing the development of government through Hebrew, Greek, and Roman history and comparing Franklin Roosevelt to Emperor Diocletian. Uncle Kit was clearly an autodidact.

The letters reveal scattered facts about his life. In one he says that after leaving the army he "bore arms as a free lance" in Guatemala and Mexico. In another he refers to working as a timekeeper and stenographer on railroad construction jobs, as a sheepherder in Wyoming, Colorado, Idaho, Montana, Utah, Nevada, California, Oregon, and Washington, and as a farmhand in

Arizona, New Mexico, Texas, and Oklahoma, "farming for my keep." In 1934, he says, he "drifted for self-preservation" to the federal transient camp in Oklahoma City, and then to camps in Fort Smith, Texarkana, Austin, and San Antonio, where he subsisted on a two-dollar-a-week allowance "waiting for the job offered by the New Deal" until he was hired by the refinery in Southton. However, shortly after his correspondence with my father started, the refinery closed down and he moved into a boarding house in San Antonio, living on his old age assistance check of twenty-six dollars a month plus the ten dollars a month that my father was sending him.

None of Uncle Kit's letters show any regrets for his way of life. In one he writes, "It would be useless to tell you of all the opportunities I let slip, but I will add, these were thrown away because I always imagined there were better opportunities further on." In another he speaks of his "natural (or perhaps unnatural) proclivity to wanderlust, instilled in me and aggravated by father's insistence on my following explicitly his policies rather than compromising on some of my own wishes." In response to my father's offer to send him some reading material while he was still working at Southton, he wrote, "I have some very good books which give me company in the evenings and my wages are sufficient to give me plenty to eat. What more do we get from life?" He apparently never married. In one letter he congratulated my father for having done so, saying, "I would have been far less restless and better off had I married."

The last letter in the package is dated from San Antonio in October 1941. In it Uncle Kit speaks of corresponding with a lawyer in Dallas about his sister's estate. My father told me that a month after receiving that letter he got one from the sheriff in Uvalde, saying that Uncle Kit had died in a hotel there and a letter from my father was found in his suitcase. His burial insurance paid for his funeral. My father never knew why he had gone to

Uvalde.

Uncle Kit was a lifelong drifter, the "Forgotten Man at the bottom of the economic pyramid" that Franklin Roosevelt spoke about. Were it not for the packet of old letters, he would have dropped between the cracks of history.

November 17, 2011

✥ 3 ✥

A LOVE STORY

T**HE PLYMOUTH COLONY** had Priscilla Mullins and John Alden ("Why don't you speak for yourself, John?") and Jamestown had Pocahontas and John Smith, even though Pocahontas married someone else and went to England and had her portrait painted wearing a funny neck ruff, but Texas has no great love story among its founding myths. Stephen F. Austin was a bachelor, and Sam Houston, before he came to Texas, had an unhappy first marriage that lasted eleven weeks. Houston's middle-aged marriage to Margaret Lea could hardly be described as a passionate romance—after all, his mother-in-law lived with them, and the staid *Handbook of Texas* says that Margaret "served as a restraining influence" on her free-wheeling husband. They did, however, produce eight children.

Of the rest of Texas's founding fathers, Anson Jones never married, and David Burnett waited until he was forty-two to marry, and that was in New Jersey. Who could have a passionate romance in New Jersey? Mirabeau Lamar, the second president of the Republic of Texas, came to Texas as a widower and, like Houston, married again in middle age, when he was "on the shady side of fifty-three," as he said in a poem addressed to his bride. Lamar comes closer than any of our Texas heroes to being a romantic lover, at least on paper. He was a prolific poet, and he addressed innumerable poems to various women in his life, both by name and under sobriquets such as "the Jenny Lind of Georgia" and "the minstrel maiden of Mobile." However, it seems that his advances were often rebuffed. In a poem entitled

"There Is a Maid I Dearly Love" he wrote: *I have long been her worshipper / And evermore must be / Yet colder far than Zembia's snows / That maiden is to me.*

The absence of a genuine love story in Texas's past means that in order to write a Valentine's Day column I am going to have to turn to the story of my own parents' courtship and marriage. It is a story that I learned in bits and pieces while I was growing up, but only got the full details of from a package of letters I found in my mother's trunk after her death. As a child I knew that my parents were married in Seymour, Texas, in May 1932, and that their marriage was a happy one. What I did not know until I started reading the letters my father wrote to my mother during their courtship was that they had first met in the spring of 1929, when my mother was teaching high school in Nocona, Texas, and my father was a young engineer with the federal government's Public Roads Administration in Fort Worth. The letters show that they immediately fell in love, and that by the fall of 1929 they had decided to get married but had not yet told their parents. Then came the stock market crash of October 29, 1929, and the ensuing Great Depression. My mother's father, who owned a drug store in Nocona, lost his business and his savings, and my mother's school-teacher's salary became a necessary contribution to her family's finances. She did not feel that she could leave her teaching job to get married, and she knew that if she got married she could not get another teaching job, since schools did not hire married women as teachers in those days. So for two years they visited back and forth between her parents' home and his, going to movies and plays together and writing each other about how much they missed each other between dates.

Finally, in the spring of 1932, the superintendent of the Nocona schools announced that there was not enough money in the county treasury to pay all of the teachers in the fall, and some would be let go. My mother was the youngest teacher in the high school, and she knew that she would not be hired again in the fall, so she wrote to my father and told him that she would accept the proposal he had repeated on every date for the past two years.

I learned about their wedding day over dinner on their sixtieth wedding anniversary. In the 1930s in Texas, a groom had to obtain a marriage license in the county where the wedding was to take place, three days before the wedding. My parents were to be married in Seymour, where my mother's parents had moved, but my father could not take time off from work to drive from Fort Worth to Seymour to get the license, so my grandfather offered to arrange it for him, with the understanding that my father would go to the courthouse with him and pick it up the morning of the wedding. When they got to the courthouse my father produced a ten-dollar bill to pay the two-dollar license fee, only to be told that there was no change in the courthouse for ten dollars. My grandfather wrote a check for two dollars, and he and my father went across the street to the florist to get the bridal bouquet. That cost five dollars, and again my father pulled out his ten-dollar bill. The florist sent it up and down the main street of Seymour to be changed, but no store in Seymour had change for ten dollars in the till. Again my grandfather wrote a check, and my father put the bill in an envelope and gave it to the minister after the ceremony. The next day the newspaper carried a long account of the wedding, describing my mother's dress and the bridesmaids' dresses and concluding with a single line about my father: "The groom is a prosperous young businessman from Fort Worth." That, my father said, was because he was the only person in Baylor County who had ten dollars.

I learned something else at that anniversary dinner. My parents were progressive young people with modern ideas about marriage, and mother told me that she persuaded the minister who married them to alter the traditional wedding vows in order to provide for the possibility of divorce. Instead of promising each other to wed "until death do us part," my parents agreed to marriage "as long as our love shall last." It lasted all of their lives, and I think that's a pretty good Valentine's Day story.

February 12, 2009

✣ 4 ✣

FIGGI

TWO WEEKS AGO I drove to San Antonio to say goodbye to my friend Figgi Rosengren, whose memorial service was held on May 5. Figgi was eighty-three when he died, and he led the fullest of lives, but his death diminished the lives of everyone who knew him because being around him was so much fun.

I first met Figgi, whose real name was Frank, when I moved to San Antonio in 1966. I had temporarily rented a room in the Crocket Hotel, just behind the Alamo. Figgi's mother's bookstore, Rosengren's, was on the ground floor of the hotel. Rosengren's was a Texas institution, and had been since 1935, when Figgi's parents moved the store from Chicago to San Antonio. Figgi's father had died before I discovered the store, and his mother Florence was running it. Florence had a genius for getting to know her customers and matching them with books. Someone would come in the front door and Florence would say, "Oh, a book just came in that I know you will like," and they would go out with the book in hand. When I moved to the country in 1970, Florence picked out a small library to get me through long winter nights: it included Tolstoy's *War and Peace*; Montaigne's *Essays*; and Burton's *Anatomy of Melancholy*.

Figgi grew up in a bookish atmosphere, surrounded by what San Antonio had to offer in the way of Bohemian society—supplemented by visiting literati, who always called at the bookstore and frequently ended up at the Rosengren home for dinner. He published his first play, "The Nuts of the Roundtable," at the age of ten, and went on in the 1950s to become a promising young New

York playwright, living in Greenwich Village with his wife, Cam, and writing plays for the legitimate theater and screenplays for television while holding down a day job as a television producer. By the time I met them, he and Cam had moved back to San Antonio, where he was helping public television station KLRN get off the ground.

In those years Figgi was clean shaven, but as he grew older he sported a Lincolnesque beard, which with his upswept eyebrows and his wide smile made him look like an aging imp. When he laughed, his eyes sparkled and he laughed all over, just like a baby. Figgi and Cam's house was always full of young people in their twenties looking for advice on how to get into show business, or seeking a good dinner, or just letting Figgi's enthusiasm for life rub off on them. At the memorial service a man in his sixties, a successful actor, stood up and told how, as a young man, he had returned to San Antonio from a year in Mexico, broke and discouraged, and had dropped in to the see Cam and Figgi. They invited him to stay to dinner, and then to spend the night, and then to move into their spare room. He stayed six months, and no one ever suggested to him that he should move on.

In the 1970s, Figgi and Cam moved into the house his parents had bought in 1935, a rammed-earth cottage on the banks of the San Antonio River built in the late eighteenth century. It is at the end of a dead-end street that leads off River Road, and it is a world in itself. Figgi's parents had entertained people like John Dos Passos, Robert Frost, Rockwell Kent, and Bennett Cerf there, and he and Cam kept up that tradition. You never knew whom you would meet there, but you were always sure to have a good time. Once my wife and I dropped by to find Jaston Williams, cocreator and costar of *Greater Tuna*, visiting. Williams kept us all in stitches for several hours, talking about his childhood in Dell City and Van Horn and his brother Corky Williams, a short, fast fellow whom Williams described as Van Horn High School's secret weapon on the football field—his technique was to head-butt opposing players in the stomach. Corky had a wild hair as a young man. Williams told us that several years ago he was having dinner with Corky in a Fort Worth restaurant when a man walked over to their table and said, "Aren't you Corky Williams?" Corky allowed that he was, and the man asked, "Are you the same Corky Williams that was found naked in the lobby of the Blackstone Hotel during the Fat Stock Show in 1959?" According to Jaston, Corky paused a minute and said, "Rings a bell."

Figgi himself was a superb raconteur. Many of his stories revolved around the well-known people in the theatrical world, not because he was a name-dropper, but because he cherished creative people and creative people tend to become famous. I once asked him how he came to be called Figgi, and he said, "Do you want to hear the short version or the version with Mrs. Patrick Campbell in it?" Mrs. Patrick Campbell was a famous English actress of the 1920s, so of course I said I wanted to hear that version. Figgi said that when he was an infant his parents put him in the window of the Chicago bookshop every day, building a playpen out of books around him. Mrs. Patrick Campbell came into the shop one day and asked who the baby in the window was, and Frank Rosengren explained that it was his son. "Well," Mrs. Campbell said, "I hope his name is Felix because he is the happiest baby I have ever seen." Young Frank became Felix to his parents, and when he started to talk he could not say "Felix" but called himself Figgi.

Figgi told stories with impeccable theatrical timing, and he told them that way right to the end. His daughter, Emily, told me that a few nights before he died he was sitting in his wheelchair on the screened porch with some friends who had brought a picnic supper, and for some reason the talk turned to Murphy beds, the folding beds that were popular furnishings in small apartments in the 1920s. Figgi was nodding in his chair, half asleep, when someone asked if he remembered Murphy beds. Suddenly, the actor was back on stage. "Do I remember Murphy beds?" Figgi said. "I slept with Mrs. Murphy!" Then a two-second pause, followed by, "And she smiled."

There were one hundred and fifty people at the memorial service, which was held under the trees in Figgi and Cam's yard. Jim Cullum's Happy Jazz Band played, and there was plenty of champagne. It was a great send-off for Figgi, but everyone there wished he hadn't gone.

May 20, 2010

✤ 5 ✤

RACHEL ON THE RADIO

RACHEL OSIER LINDLEY introduced me to Frankie "Half-Pint" Jaxon and His Quarts of Joy and changed my life, or at least the Wednesday evening portion of it. Lindley hosts a radio program called *Old Timey* on KRTS, the public radio station in Marfa, every Wednesday night from 8:00 to 9:00 p.m. I have started rushing through dinner on Wednesday nights so that I can get the dishes washed and get into the living room in time to see what she will come up with next.

Lindley is fascinated with the odd corners of popular music that were recorded between 1910 and 1950. We are not talking about mainstream performers like Guy Lombardo and Glenn Miller, or even the John Philip Sousa Band. We are talking about people like Half-Pint Jaxon, a diminutive African American sometime female impersonator who started off with a song-and-dance act in vaudeville in the 1920s, and ended up performing at Harlem's Apollo Theater with Bessie Smith, Ethel Waters, and the Harlem Hamfats. Jaxon specialized in male-female dialogues with funky jazz backgrounds in which he did both voices. One of his recordings played by Lindley, "The Mortgage Blues," is not a blues at all, but a weird combination of an African American toast and a call-and-response piece with the rhythm of a jump-rope rhyme that goes on for six minutes; I have never heard anything like it in my life. Jaxon disappeared from the stage in 1940, but left a couple of dozen recordings behind him. Lindley discovered him when she and her husband, Chase, bought a box of 78 RPM records on eBay; one of them was a Half-Pint Jaxon recording. She began researching Jaxon and found that an Austrian company, Document Records, had produced a CD of his surviving recordings. That is what she was playing on the air the night I heard him.

Lindley says she enjoys the challenge of researching little-known recording artists from the vaudeville, burlesque, and medicine-show traditions, as well as early blues and jazz performers, jug bands, and spiritual and gospel groups. She has discovered a network of record collectors like Joe Bussard, an old-time string-band enthusiast who has thousands of 78s in the basement of his Frederick, Maryland, home and puts out digitally remastered versions of them on his Old Hat CDs. Lindley is somewhat in awe of people like Bussard. "I'm an enthusiast, not an expert," she says. But talking to her it is clear that she has done her own research, and she incorporates this research into her programs, giving tantalizing information about the artists whose work she is playing—such as the fact that Half-Pint Jaxon stood five foot two and worked at the Pentagon during World War II, or that South Carolina medicine-show performer Pink Anderson's first name was appropriated by the 1960s rock band Pink Floyd (the Floyd came from Floyd Council, a North Carolina bluesman).

"There is a mystery to old records," Lindley told me. "I'm interested in the stories of the people who made them. It seems as though bands today are marketers as well as musicians, and all musicians have to spend as much time promoting themselves as they do playing music. I'm interested in the people back in the bayous with no teeth and no training, who just played their music to small audiences and then were found by record companies."

Lindley told me that she first learned about old-time music while taking a course in the history of rock and roll at the University of Texas in 2002. "I thought I could listen to Talking Heads and get a grade for it," she said, "but it turned out that the teacher was an expert on the history of radio and the recording industry, and he made us listen to all these records from the 1920s. I loved it!" She added, "We never got to rock and roll."

Lindley's other love, besides old-time music, is radio. As a child growing up in the Chicago suburb of Riverside, she and her best friend used to amuse themselves by recording imaginary radio shows on her tape deck. She started working in real radio at the age of sixteen, at Riverside-Brookfield High School, which had its own radio station that broadcast over a loudspeaker system into classrooms. "We weren't really on the air," she told me, "but we had a board and microphones." She and a friend produced a rock and roll program that was broadcast every morning before classes started.

At the University of Texas at Austin, where Lindley majored in photojournalism, she worked at the campus student-run radio station, KVRX, which advertises that it plays music you won't hear anywhere else—"none of the hits, all of the time." Lindley was program director there for two years, and it clearly left its mark on her. In her senior year she was also an intern at KUT, the University's National Public Radio affiliate, and that is how she first heard about KRTS, Marfa's fledgling public radio station. She moved to Marfa in 2006 to work as an intern at KRTS.

"I had always wanted to live in a small town and work at a radio station," she told me, "but in college I didn't think working at a radio station was something you could do when you grew up. I planned to come to Marfa for the summer and then move back to Chicago, so that if I failed miserably at being an adult my parents would feed me." Instead, Lindley married her college boyfriend and they have become an integral part of Marfa life. Lindley is a full-time employee at KRTS and helps to run the station; her husband works for a local landscape firm and stands in as a maître d' at Cochineal Restaurant one night a week. Few people are able to fulfill their life's ambition at twenty-five. And few people have made such a contribution to their adopted community in such a short time.

Old Timey. Every Wednesday night at 8:00 p.m.

October 10, 2009

✤ 6 ✤

THE LADY LIBRARIANS

MY FRIEND Michael Baskin from Denver was in town not long ago and dropped by our house to visit. Mike is a lawyer and a bibliophile. As an undergraduate at the University of Texas at Austin, he worked for Miss Katherine Blow in the Humanities Reference Library, so it was natural that our talk turned to the remarkable women who were the mainstays of the University of Texas library system fifty years ago.

Those women were all what we then called "maiden ladies," unmarried women who remained slightly over forty for several decades. They were smart women from small Texas towns where teaching, nursing, and librarianship were the only professions open to them. Today they would be corporation presidents. As it was they ran the library system of a major American university and did it superbly. Three in particular stand out in memory, because each made a unique contribution to Texas history: Miss Fannie Ratchford in the Miriam Lutcher Stark Rare Books Library; Miss Winnie Allen in the University Archives; and Dr. Nettie Lee Benson in the Latin American Collection.

Miss Fannie Ratchford was born in Paint Rock in 1887. She entered the University of Texas in 1905 and graduated in 1919. It took her fourteen years to earn a BA because she had to drop out and teach school in order to earn the money to continue her education. When she finally graduated, she joined the University's library system while she worked on a master's degree, and stayed there until she retired in 1957. She achieved a world-wide scholarly reputation for her publications on the works of Charlotte and Emily Brontë and the literary forgeries of Thomas J. Wise, but she is best remembered at the University for her introduction of the custom of morning and afternoon tea in the Stark Library or, on pleasant days, on the hedge-lined terrace outside. Morning tea was at 10:00 a.m. and afternoon tea at 4:00 p.m., and in the summertime the afternoon tea was iced and flavored with mint that Ratchford grew in a pot on the terrace.

In the mid-1930s, Ratchford got interested in Texas architecture and decided that she should make a record of houses built in Texas before the Civil War. I have never been able to learn what motivated her, as the subject was far from her scholarly interest. At the time, she neither drove nor had she ever used a camera. She bought a Leica and taught herself to use it, and she bought a Chrysler Airflow sedan and hired a young woman to drive it. She and her driver went all over East Texas photographing and making notes on structures ranging from log cabins to antebellum mansions, many of them in deplorable condition. Unlike her research into nineteenth-century English literature, Ratchford's architectural notes and photographs were never published. Today they are in the Texas State Archives, and they are an invaluable record of Texas's built heritage, much of which has vanished since Ratchford made her trips into East Texas.

Miss Winnie Allen was a native of Henrietta, where she graduated from high school in 1917. She went on to the University of Texas, interrupting her academic career several times to teach school, and received her master's degree in 1925. She immediately went to work as an assistant in the University of Texas Archives, which at that time consisted of the Stephen F. Austin papers and about twenty other collections, mostly Spanish documents relating to the history of Texas. In 1936 she became the chief archivist, a position she held for thirty-five years. She built the University of Texas Archives into one of the major depositories in the United States for material relating to the history of the Southwest; when she retired in 1960 it contained about four thousand collections.

But Allen made another contribution to Texas history. Her

thinking about historical evidence went far beyond the documents and letters normally found in archives—she was a pioneer in the use of oral history—and in 1952 she circulated a paper entitled "A Tentative Plan for a State Program of Texas Life" among her colleagues and friends. In it she called for the creation of a state agency to coordinate all efforts to locate and preserve records relating to Texas history, including historic buildings and landscapes, and for a privately-funded foundation to support the agency's efforts. She sent it not only to academics but to politicians and influential businessmen and then peppered them with letters about it. Governor Alan Shivers was so impressed with the idea that in 1953 he got the legislature to pass a bill establishing the Texas State Historical Survey Committee, which launched an inventory of historic structures in the state and started a program to record and mark them. That committee eventually became the Texas Historical Commission, which is now the state's major preservation agency and a model for preservation agencies in other states.

Miss Nettie Lee Benson was born in 1905 and grew up in Sinton, in South Texas, surrounded by people who spoke Spanish. She fell in love with the Spanish language and Mexican culture at an early age. Like Ratchford and Allen, she had to drop out of the University of Texas and teach school to make ends meet, but she taught at the Instituto Inglés-Español, a Methodist school in Monterrey, Mexico. She earned a master's degree in Latin American history in 1935 and a doctorate in 1949. In 1942, just after starting on her doctorate, she took a job in what was then called the Garcia Collection of the University of Texas Library, a collection of manuscripts and printed items relating to Mexican history purchased from the estate of the Mexican bibliophile Genaro Garcia. Benson developed an aggressive acquisition strategy for the collection and traveled all over Mexico, South America, and the Caribbean buying material for it. By the time she retired in 1975, it had grown from thirty thousand volumes to three hundred thousand and had been named for her: the Nettie Lee Benson Latin American Collection.

Benson built a great library, and that library may have made the greatest contribution of all to the study of Texas history. It enabled scholars to see Texas through Mexican as well as Anglo American eyes, and to shift their viewpoint from one of standing in the east looking west to one of standing in the south looking north. And when you do that, you see things differently.

Miss Ratchford, Miss Allen, and Miss Benson all had three things in common. They came from small towns, they were smart, and they were determined. That carried them each a long way.

May 12, 2011

✥ 7 ✥

AMELIA WILLIAMS,
COTTON FARMER AND SCHOLAR

L AST WEEKEND I had a brush
with the past—my own family's
past and Texas's past, too. My wife and I drove over to Cameron, a
county-seat town northeast of Austin, for a ceremony honoring
Amelia Williams. It seems that a local foundation in Cameron, the
Yoe Foundation, selects half a dozen or so distinguished natives of
Milam County each year and places plaques honoring them and
their achievements in the Cameron high school. Cousin Amelia,
as I was brought up to call her, was born in Milam County in 1876
and taught history at the University of Texas from 1925 to 1951.
Her doctoral dissertation, which she completed in 1931, was entitled "A Critical Study of the Siege of the Alamo and of the
Personnel of Its Defenders." It was the first scholarly study of that
battle, and for many years was the only source for the list of the
men who died there. In fact, Cousin Amelia provided the names
of the Alamo heroes that are carved in stone on Pompeo Coppini's
imposing monument on Alamo Plaza in San Antonio. Of course,
no such list is ever complete, even though it is carved in stone, and
other scholars have added to and even subtracted from Cousin
Amelia's list of 181 defenders. One of the most recent writers on
the subject, a former US Army criminal investigator named
Thomas Ricks Lindley, devotes an entire chapter to a vehement
attack on Cousin Amelia's list in his book, *Alamo Traces* (Lanham,
Maryland: Republic of Texas Press, 2003). Lindley argues that
Williams purposely undercounted the number of defenders and
accuses her of "misrepresentation, alteration, and fabrication of

data." I get the impression that, had cousin Amelia been in the army with Lindley, he would have had her court-martialed and probably shot. Fortunately they were not contemporaries, Lindley being only fifteen when Cousin Amelia died in 1958.

I don't remember Cousin Amelia as a misrepresenter or fabricator of anything, only as a nice old lady with her silver hair in braids who was my grandmother's cousin and who gave me an inscribed copy of one of her books, *Following General Sam Houston*, when I was seven. She also was the coeditor, with Eugene Barker, of Sam Houston's papers. She once told my father that she was going to write a book about Sam Houston that would make her a lot of money because it would have a lot of sex in it, but she died before getting around to it.

One of the people at the Cameron ceremony was Todd Hansen, whose new book, *The Alamo Reader* (Mechanicsburg, Pennsylvania: The Stackpole Press, 2003) is an eight-hundred-page compilation of source material on the Alamo and a must for every Alamo buff. Hansen told me some things about Cousin Amelia that I did not know, and I think they are worth passing on. Her father, Thomas Herbert Williams, was an ex-Confederate soldier who came to Texas after the Civil War. He bought a two-thousand-acre plantation in Milam County, married a local girl, and had five children, of whom Cousin Amelia, born in 1876, was the oldest. The other four, all girls, were named Harriet Emily, South Carolina, Julia Emma, and Virginia Kentucky. Thomas Herbert died when Amelia was fourteen and her youngest sister was three. His wife died eight years later, and Cousin Amelia was left at the age of twenty-two to manage the plantation and look after her younger sisters. She wrote farm contracts, oversaw tenants, sold the crops, cooked, sewed, gardened, put up preserves, killed and dressed hogs, and saw that all of her sisters finished high school and graduated from college. Somehow, she found the time and energy to graduate from Southwest Texas State Normal College, and for fifteen years between 1910 and 1925 she taught in the rural grammar schools of Milam County.

Finally, in 1925, she entered graduate school at the University of Texas and chose the Alamo as her dissertation topic. She searched the records of the General Land office in Austin for the names of people who had been given a land grant because a husband or father had been killed at the Alamo, and then she drove a Model T Ford all over Texas persuading their descendants to look into their attics for letters, diaries, and other documents that might throw light on the battle. She tracked down and interviewed the grandchildren of Susanna Dickenson, one of the few Alamo survivors, who told her the stories about the siege that their grandmother had told them. Finally, in June 1931, she defended her dissertation and was awarded the doctorate. She was fifty-five years old. She went on to have a productive teaching and writing career at the university that lasted for twenty more years. Folks who are considering a second career in middle age might profit from her example.

Part of our day's program in Cameron was to share a picnic lunch at the old Williams home place with a few other relatives and the Hansens. Cousin Amelia never married, but her three surviving nieces, ladies in their eighties, were there, along with some younger family members. The house, a rambling, two-story frame building with upstairs and downstairs galleries across its front, is surrounded by fields and pastures. It has not been occupied in thirty years, but the nieces maintain it for annual family reunions. While we lunched on crustless ham salad and cheese sandwiches, one of them told me that my grandmother had often visited there when she was a young woman, and that one Christmas week she and her cousins had written their names on a window pane in the parlor with a diamond ring that one of the girls had received as an engagement ring—they wanted to see if the diamond was real.

She gestured toward the window and I went over to look at it. Sure enough, there on the pane were the words, "Sue Border and Amelia Williams, January 2, 1897." Cousin Amelia died in 1958, and my grandmother ten years later, but here was a record of friendship that had survived both of them. Seeing it was the high point of the trip for me.

November 26, 2003

✤ 8 ✤

THOROUGHLY MODERN MOJELLA

MOJELLA MOORE of Alpine is a cosmopolitan, sophisticated, and beautiful woman of eighty-one who lives in a ten-room, ranch-style house north of town. Her living room has wall-to-wall carpeting and is furnished with comfortable easy chairs, couches, and a flat-screen television set. Her ample kitchen is equipped with a refrigerator, a dishwasher, and an electric stove. She is firmly planted in the twenty-first century. She was wearing slacks and a chic top the day I visited with her. She is a modern woman.

But Mojella (she was named after a character in Helen Hunt Jackson's novel *Ramona*) Moore spent her childhood in the nineteenth century, even though she was born in 1929. Her first home was a one-room adobe house on the O Ranch, northwest of Candelaria and below the Candelaria Rim, where her parents, Joe Bailey and Edith Rogers, raised goats. Her father added an adobe screened porch to the front of the house, with canvas flaps that could be lowered, and that porch served as a bedroom for Moore, her two brothers, her parents, the schoolteacher that occasionally boarded with them, and "whatever strays came along," she said. The other room was furnished with a wood cook stove, a table and some chairs, and some cabinets. There was no electricity. A fireplace provided heat, and kerosene lamps gave light after dark. Moore told me that once, during the Depression, her family went for a year without going into town. She said during that time she asked her mother if they were poor and her mother said, "No, we're not poor at all. We just don't have any money."

However, they had goats, which were kept "under herd,"

meaning that goat herders with dogs tended the goats from camps on the ranch. The herders were usually from Mexico, and would spend six months or so in their camp and then go home for a month, to be replaced by a friend or relative. The goats were Angoras. They were hair goats, not meat goats, and were raised for their fleece. "As far as I know, we never ate a goat," Moore told me. The goats were driven to the ranch corral and sheared twice a year by a traveling gang of shearers, and that was about the only out-of-the-ordinary event in the young Mojella Moore's life. "It was an occasion I really looked forward to," she said. The half-dozen shearers, their boss, a cook, and a swamper—a man-of-all-work— brought a gasoline-powered shearing machine, to which mechanical clippers were hooked up. It took about ten minutes to shear each goat, and the shearers were paid by the goat. Moore recalled that the boss handed each man a lead token when he had sheared a goat, and the tokens were redeemed for cash when the shearing was finished. There was work for Moore and her brothers, too; they combed the burrs out of the goats' fleece before the shearers got to them.

Moore's family eventually moved from the O Ranch to the nearby Dow Ranch, and she remembers driving herds of goats on horseback up the Candelaria Rim to the Brite Ranch, where they were loaded into trucks. She told me that she rode horseback as a baby, sitting on the saddle in front of her mother, and by the time she was five she could ride by herself. "I learned to ride on a horse named Dunny," she said. "Dunny taught several aunts and uncles and my brothers to ride, and he taught me, too."

In 1948, Moore married Ed Moore, who was a river rider for the Department of Agriculture, trying to prevent Mexican cattle infected with hoof-and-mouth disease from crossing the Rio Grande into Texas. The river riders worked in pairs, each man patrolling an eleven-mile stretch of river each day. One went upstream from their camp, one went downstream, and the next day they switched. The Moores' first married home was a tent at Porvenir, up the river from Candelaria. "It was a government tent," Moore said, "but it was better than the adobe house the other rider lived in."

Ed and Mojella Moore eventually built a store on the Juan Prieto Ranch between Candelaria and Ruidosa, and Mojella ran the store. "We sold everything—groceries, candy, clothes, everything," she told me. "Ninety percent of our customers came from across the river. We had a beer joint in the back room—that was prerequisite in those days—and that was where the river riders gathered." There was no electricity in the store, but they kept the beer cold in a butane refrigerator.

The Moores bought candelilla wax at the store. Because the Mexican government had a monopoly on the purchase of the wax in Mexico and set an artificially low price on it, much of the wax gathered in Chihuahua was smuggled across the river and sold on the American side. "Many a time I took a bobtail truck down the river to meet my wax men," Moore told me. "I would take the wax to the US Customs station at Presidio to declare it and then go to the bank in Ojinaga to get pesos to pay the wax men. They would lie out in the brush on the Texas side until I got back." The bank in Ojinaga, she recalled, was a one-room affair with a counter across the middle, entered through an unmarked door in a wall near the plaza.

While Moore was running the store, her widowed mother managed Kingston Hot Springs, now Chinati Hot Springs. There was no electricity there, either. Visitors paid twenty-five cents for a bath in the springs, and they could rent a cabin for ten dollars a week. The cabins were furnished with kerosene stoves.

In 1956, Moore moved completely into the twentieth century. She and her husband opened a feed store in Alpine, Moore's General Store, and she worked behind the counter while her husband hauled cattle in an International semi-trailer truck with removable sides. She recalled that the local ranchers all gathered in the coffee shop at the Holland Hotel at 5:00 a.m., and that was where cattle deals, including hauling contracts, were made. If you weren't there, you just missed out. The Moores closed the feed store in 1981 and opened a self-storage business, which Mojella Moore, now a widow, still manages. She is a thoroughly modern lady.

January 13, 2010

✢ 9 ✢

FRUGALITY WAS A VIRTUE

MOST OF THE first generation of big West Texas
ranchers, the ones who built the mansions that lined Summit
Avenue in Fort Worth when I was growing up there, had gone
through the hard times that followed the Civil War. Many of them
were notoriously close with a dollar. My grandmother used to say
that some of them would skin a flea for the hide and tallow.

There is a story that illustrates this. Dan Waggoner grew up on
a hardscrabble farm in Tennessee, came out to Texas as a young
man in the 1850s, and by the 1880s had accumulated a fortune in
land and cattle. He built a stone mansion on a hill just south of
Decatur, Texas. Like most ranchers in the area, he let his horse
herd graze on the open range in the winter and rounded them up
and brought them home in the early spring. One spring a neigh-
boring rancher was gathering his horses and ran across several of
Waggoner's. He put them in his herd, thinking that he would do
Waggoner a favor and have his men drop them off as they went
through Decatur. When they got to the Waggoner ranch they
penned the herd and showed Waggoner his horses. He thanked
them and asked them to catch them and stake them near a little
creek close to the house. They did and then asked permission to
camp overnight by the creek, which Waggoner granted. There
were some shallots growing in a garden near the creek, and the
cowboys asked Waggoner if they could have a few to flavor their
supper that night. He told them to go ahead and pull some up,
which they did. The next morning when they were breaking camp
Waggoner came down and said, "I guess I'll have to charge you
boys a nickel for those shallots."

In another version it was watercress growing along the creek that the men were charged for, but the result was the same. Every cowboy in West Texas heard the story, and no one ever caught a stray horse for Dan Waggoner again.

It was Dan Waggoner's son, Tom Waggoner, who built an office building in downtown Fort Worth in the 1920s and opened the Arlington Downs race track in nearby Arlington. The Waggoner Building had a barber shop in it, but Tom Waggoner preferred to go over to the somewhat tonier Texas Hotel to get his haircuts. One day, however, he was in a hurry, and he ducked into the shop in his own building. When the barber was finished Waggoner asked how much he owed him, and the man said, "Well, Mr. Waggoner, when your boys come in here they usually give me a dollar." Waggoner's reply was, "I don't have a rich daddy like they do. Here's a quarter."

My friend Jim Bratcher of Bulverde likes to tell about a wealthy sheep rancher in San Angelo named Shannon, who had a famous flock of bred-up sheep. Sometime in the late 1890s, a man and his sister were on their way to Shannon's ranch in a buggy, intending to buy some sheep from him. They did not know Shannon, and they planned to ask for the sheep on credit. As Bratcher puts it, they were a little elevated in manner. On their way they met a shabbily-dressed old man, also traveling, at a water-hole where they set up camp for the night. The next morning they told the old man that they would pay him a dollar if he would catch up and hitch their horses. He did so and they paid him and continued on their way. When they got to their destination, they discovered that the old man who had taken their dollar was Shannon himself. Uppity and careless with a dollar as they were, they did not get their sheep on credit.

J. Frank Dobie continues the story in his book *Cow People*. This same Mr. Shannon was chastised by his banker for the way he dressed when he came into town from the ranch. He would come into the bank wearing torn Levis and a dirty shirt, looking like something the rats had dragged in. Finally the banker told him, "Mr. Shannon, you are one of the wealthiest men in West Texas. Everyone respects you. The way you dress does not suit your station in life. Why don't you go over to the store and shell out a few dollars for a good suit, some clean shirts and collars, and a good hat? You ought to dress in a more respectable fashion when you come to town." "You mean here in San Angelo?" Shannon asked. "Yes, of course," the banker said. "Well," Shannon replied, "Everyone here in town knows me and knows who I am. What difference does it make how I dress?"

A few months later the same banker was in Kansas City and he met Shannon on the sidewalk. Shannon had ridden in a caboose behind a trainload of steers he was shipping, and had slept in the Kansas City stockyards to save money on a hotel. He looked like a tramp. The banker was horrified. "Mr. Shannon," he said, "I am embarrassed for you. You have just sold a trainload of steers. Why don't you go to a store and buy some clean clothes? You should be dressed like a respectable ranchman." "You mean here in Kansas City?" Shannon asked. "Yes, sir, here in Kansas City and everywhere you go," the banker said. "Well," Shannon said, "I don't know anyone in Kansas City and no one here knows me. What difference does it make how I dress?"

The tight-fistedness of Texas ranchers may have been responsible for populating Montana and Wyoming with Texas cowboys. It was a common complaint among the men who went up the trail to Kansas in the 1870s and '80s that Texas outfits fed their hands nothing but cornbread, sowbelly, and beans. Ranches in the mountain states stocked their chuckwagons with expensive delicacies like canned tomatoes, canned peaches, and wheat flour for pancakes and biscuits. Teddy Blue Abbot claimed that was why so many Texas cowboys stayed there to work instead of coming back home, in spite of nearly freezing to death in the winter—the grub was so much better. Texas cowboys were the best in the world, and so those northern ranchers' generosity with the groceries paid off in the long run.

July 30, 2009

✤ 10 ✤

APACHE ADAMS

APACHE ADAMS is not a typical Big Bend cowboy, but he
is the quintessential Big Bend Cowboy, having an excess of the
qualities that turn a good cowboy into a superlative one. He is a
fine horseman, a superb roper, and he has no back-down, to use
his own phrase (which he employs about someone else, not himself). He has broken fingers, arms, legs, a collarbone, a hip, and a
pelvis trying to get a job done, and has worked with those bones
broken until he accomplished what he set out to do, whether it was
roping a bull or trying to get a trailer off high center. Adams is a
man who is completely devoid of quitting sense. As Don Cadden,
who has just written a book about Adams called *Tied Hard and
Fast: Apache Adams, Big Bend Cowboy* (Denver: Outskirts Press,
2011), told me, "People say Apache's done crazy things but when
all else fails they call him."

Don Cadden's book about Adams should be required reading
for any young person who thinks they might want to be a cowboy.
There is no romance in it, but there is a lot of hard and dangerous
work. The book could have been titled *Wrecks I Have Been In*,
because many of Adams's stories end in situations that either
involve personal injury or miss it by a lasso's breadth. But some of
them are hilarious. Here is a sample: Adams is working cattle with
his son and a friend. The friend is using Adams's good saddle. The
friend ropes a big bull, but he has forgotten to tighten the saddle's
cinch and so when his horse puts on the brakes he and the saddle
go right over the horse's head, "like you'd squirt a seed out of a
prune," Adams says. The friend has tied his lasso hard and fast, so
Adams's good saddle is now bouncing along behind the bull.

Adams tries to rope the bull, but every time he gets close enough to throw, the saddle bounces up and his horse shies off. Finally, he gives up on the bull and ropes the saddle, so now he has the bull on two ropes with the saddle in between. His son gets another rope on the bull, but then his cinch breaks, and he and his saddle part company with his horse. Adams now has the bull, three ropes, and two saddles flopping around him. You have to buy the book to find out what happens next.

Adams was born in 1937. His parents named him Ernest Paul, but his abundant coal-black hair earned him the nickname "Apache" as a child. Apache fits in with the other somewhat peculiar Adams family names. Apache's father was Ulice Adams, and he had an uncle named Elba, and a great-uncle named Harmon. All three were ranching in the Big Bend when Apache was born. He was on a horse before he could walk, and he grew up speaking Spanish as well as English. He was definitely a child of the border. Over the years he became not only a well-respected cowboy but a well-known raconteur. He polished an inherent talent for storytelling by performing at the Alpine Cowboy Poetry Gathering.

Several years ago Adams was doing some cow work for Jeff Fort on Fort's Pinto Canyon Ranch, and Fort's wife, Marion Barthelme, gave him a tape recorder and asked him to tell his stories into it as he was driving around. She turned the tapes over to Don Cadden, and with Adams's help, Cadden organized the material on the recordings into a book in Adams's voice. One of the best parts of the narrative is Adams's Western idiom. He speaks of a corpse as being "graveyard dead." Nervous cattle are "trotty." Horses that clamp down on the bit and fail to respond to it are "cold jawing." Bulls that are "brushed up" are not especially well groomed but are hiding in the brush. Cadden has footnoted some of these terms for Eastern readers.

Adams makes a specialty of finding cattle that are brushed up. When a ranch has been sold or the lease is up and the rancher needs to move his herd elsewhere, he will hold a roundup or two and even scour the place with a helicopter, but there will always be a few wild cows that will hide out in the brush, and that is where Adams comes in. He is the cowboy of last resort. He will bring a couple of his men in and they will clear the place out. A number of the stories in Cadden's book revolve around these cow hunts. On one occasion he was called to the O2 Ranch to find out what the lessee thought were about thirty cows, which Adams agreed to gather on halves, meaning that he got to keep half of the cattle he found. When he and his men were through they had 178 cows and bulls roped and tied. Some of them had never seen a human being. Cadden says that Adams is so good at this because he is an expert tracker and "he'll rope anything."

Don Cadden is the ideal person to translate Adams's taped narratives into print. He told me that he literally had to get inside of Adams in order to do it, but he has known and worked with Adams for twenty-one years and has a way with words himself, as he is a published poet and songwriter. Cadden grew up in a rural suburb of Austin, but he fell in love with the Big Bend and cowboy life when he got a summer job as a brakeman on the Southern Pacific, working the run between Sanderson and Valentine. An Austin friend then helped him get hired for a roundup on the D Ranch in the Guadalupe Mountains one spring. "I knew enough to tell the men I was working with that I didn't know anything, and they helped me along," Cadden told me. Then, he said, he met Apache Adams at an Alpine Cowboy Poetry Gathering. He asked Adams if he could work with him, and Adams took him along on a cow hunt. "It was like going from elementary school to college in one day," Cadden told me. The two men became fast friends, and this fine book is the result of that friendship.

July 14, 2011

✦ 11 ✦

TED GRAY

THE BIG BEND lost a unique citizen when Ted Gray of Alpine died on March 14 at the age of eighty-eight. Whenever a person of Ted's age and stature in the community dies, someone will always step forward and say that the deceased was the last of his breed. Plenty of people are saying that about Ted Gray. He was not the last of his breed; there are other ranchers of his generation still around. But Ted Gray was the last of something else. He was the last man to start out in the Big Bend as a thirty-dollar-a-month cowboy and to end up owning or operating at least twenty ranches. "Back in the 1880s when land was cheap, a lot of young men did that, but it was kind of unheard of by the time I came along," he told me when I interviewed him in 2005.

Ted Gray grew up on a farm in rural Jack County, northwest of Fort Worth, in the depths of the Great Depression. He was the eleventh of twelve children. He once told me that when he was a boy he didn't know what he wanted to be, but he knew what he did not want to be and that was a farmer. A retired cowboy who had worked in the Big Bend in the 1880s told him what it was like out here. "It's cow heaven," the old man said. Ted decided he wanted to be a cowboy. At the age of fifteen, he hitched a ride on a truckload of mules going west and got off in Fort Stockton. He kept his eyes open and watched how older cowboys did things, and by the time he was twenty-one, he was a wagon boss on the Kokernot O6. He eventually became general manager of the O6. When he married and started a family, H. L. Kokernot Jr. allotted him a pasture on which to run one hundred fifty head of his own cattle, and that was the start of his career as a successful rancher.

I got to know Ted over cups of coffee at Bread and Breakfast in Alpine, one of his regular morning stops. I always learned something during those visits. Ted believed that the Davis Mountains were the best part of the Big Bend because blue grama grass, which he called "the ice cream of grasses," flourished in their volcanic soil. Good grass was the most important thing in Ted's life, because he thought good grass produced good cattle and good people. "There is a line," he told me, "that runs east and west between Marathon, Alpine, Marfa, Valentine, and Van Horn. Below that line the country is so poor that everyone who lives there has had to do something underhanded at least once in their life just to get by."

Ted had a finely-honed sense of humor. One morning, he was telling me how hard life was in Jack County during the Depression. "It was so hard people were praying for food. I remember being in church and an old farmer stood up and said, 'Lord, please bring me food for my family. Bring me a barrel of pork. Bring me a barrel of coffee, a barrel of sugar. Lord, bring me a barrel of beans.'" At that point, Ted claimed, another man stood up and said, "Lord, don't listen to that man. A barrel of beans is too many beans." I suspect that story antedates Ted by a century, but he found it funny and so do I.

I went to Ted's funeral at the Methodist church in Alpine. It was short and dignified. Every old rancher in the Big Bend was there, in a dark suit and a white hat. The Old Testament reading was the passage from Genesis about Abraham and Lot dividing up their herds. The pastor said that might seem to be an odd passage for a funeral, but she explained that Ted, who had read the Bible through twice, was very interested in Abraham. He considered him to be the first rancher, and had often tried to calculate exactly how many cattle he owned. "Now," she said, "he will be able to find that out."

Ted's older son, Ted Jr., talked about what kind of man his father was. He said that he was a successful cowboy and rancher because he valued two qualities: efficiency and thrift. He was always looking for a better and less expensive way to do things. He listed his father's skills: he could shoe a horse in fifteen minutes; he and four cowboys could brand a hundred steers in an hour; he could rope, tie, and doctor a full-grown bull all by himself; and — the ultimate accolade—he had broken thirteen bones cowboying. He also said that his father was color-blind; that if a man could do the work, it made no difference what color his skin was. He added that his father could not abide a slacker. He told a double-barreled story to illustrate both points. When Ted was manager of the O6 he and a group of cowboys were branding calves in a small pasture. They finished before lunch, and Ted told them that since they had some time on their hands they were going to fix a gap in the pasture fence before eating. Some of the men hung back behind the chuck wagon, hoping they would not be noticed, but others grabbed the tools out of the wagon and piled into Ted's pickup. Ted drove them right past the gap, out of the gate, and down the highway to Balmorhea, where there were two cafes. He went into the first one and asked the owner if he could fix chicken dinners for half a dozen hungry men. The owner said he could. Ted said, "There's just one thing. Some of them aren't white." "Oh, that's all right," the owner said. "Just tell them to go around back and we'll serve them in the kitchen." "That won't do," Ted said, and he drove everyone down to the second café, where the owner was so happy to have the business he fed everyone in the dining room.

After Ted Jr. sat down, Karen McGuire got up with a guitar and sang, "I'd Like to Be in Texas in the Spring," about an old man in a New York hotel recalling his youth in Texas. The chorus goes: *I can see the cattle grazing o'er the hills at early morn / I can see the campfires smoking at the breaking of the dawn / I was foreman of a cow ranch, a calling for a king / I'd like to be in Texas when they round up in the spring.* It was the perfect song for Ted Gray.

March 31, 2011

✤ 12 ✤

CARRY HUFFMAN AND JOE SITTER, BORDER LAWMEN

NOT LONG AGO, I spent a morning at the Marfa Sector Headquarters of the Border Patrol talking with Carry Huffman, who is the Deputy Chief Patrol Agent there. On the surface, Huffman (who pronounces his first name KO-ree) would appear to be the ultimate modern law-enforcement officer. He has been with the Border Patrol twenty-two years and has served in a number of posts, including four years in Washington, DC, and some time in South America. He is a handsome, affable man who can discuss with ease the duties and the problems of his government agency. But there is another side to Huffman, and that was what brought us together in his office. Huffman has an intense interest in the past, and especially the past of the border country that he has seen so much of as a patrol agent since he came to Marfa seven years ago.

It is Huffman's curiosity about the past that first got him interested in Joe Sitter, another border lawman who worked this area (Sitter's descendants added a final "s" to his name and he is sometimes referred to as Joe Sitters). Sitter was born in Castroville, Texas, in 1863, the son of Alsatian immigrants. He grew up in Castroville, worked as a cowboy on local ranches, and married a local girl, with whom he had three children. But when he was twenty-six, his wife died as the result of a buggy accident. Heartbroken, he gave their children to relatives to raise and struck out west by himself. He got a job as a deputy sheriff in Del Rio, where he became a local hero by helping to capture a gang of outlaws who had held up a train and were hiding out in the brush with their loot. This brought him to the attention of Texas Ranger Captain John Hughes, and when a vacancy occurred in Hughes's Company D, Hughes offered Sitter the job.

Sitter served as a Texas Ranger from August 1893 to May 1899. He married again in December 1894, and he and his wife settled down on a ranch south of Valentine, in the broken country below the Candelaria Rim that Huffman now patrols. In 1899, Sitter left the Rangers and joined the US Customs Service as a Mounted Inspector at twice his Ranger pay. It must have seemed like a good job to a man with a growing family (he and his second wife eventually had six children), but it got him involved in a feud that eventually cost him his life.

One of the most notorious smugglers in the country below the Candelaria Rim was a man called Chico Cano, who lived with his brothers across the Rio Grande at San Antonio del Bravo. There was a warrant out for his arrest in Texas, and in February 1913 Sitter and two colleagues captured him by surrounding a house where he was attending a wake and threatening to set fire to it unless he surrendered. On their way to Marfa with their prisoner, however, they were attacked by a group of Cano's men who freed Cano and wounded all three lawmen, one of them fatally. Cano later told relatives that he knew Sitter was going to kill him before they got to the Marfa jail, and he swore then that he would get Sitter before Sitter got him.

Two years later, in May 1915, Sitter led a group of lawmen into the country along the river in search of a herd of horses that had been crossed illegally into Texas, probably by Cano. With him were Customs Inspector Charley Craighead and three Texas Rangers, Eugene Hulen, Sug Cummins, and H. C. Trollinger. On the third night of the search they camped near the mouth of a box canyon, and in the night they heard horses going past and voices, one of which Sitter told his companions he recognized as Chico

Cano's. The next morning, they divided into two groups and entered the canyon. Sitter and Hulen went along a little rise on one side, and the other three men picked their way through the rocks along the other side. Suddenly, the second party was met by a hail of gunfire from the rocks ahead of them. They could see Sitter and Hulen motioning for them to go back and returning the fire. They later said that after they retreated they tried to get across the canyon to join Sitter and Hulen but were unable to do so. Finally the shooting stopped, and the three men were able to make their way to a nearby ranch, where they phoned for help. A posse arrived the next day and found Sitter and Hulen's bodies, stripped naked and bloating in the sun. Hulen had evidently been killed early in the fight, but there were sixty empty shell casings around Sitter. The decomposing bodies were loaded onto mules and taken to the Magee Ranch, where they were buried. They were later exhumed by the Marfa funeral home; Sitter was reburied in the Valentine cemetery and Hulen in his hometown of Gainesville, Texas. Hulen had enlisted in the Rangers only a few weeks before his death; he had no previous law-enforcement experience and owed his appointment to the political influence of his brother, railroad executive John A. Hulen.

Because of Sitter's prominence as a law-enforcement officer and the gruesome details surrounding the recovery of his and Hulen's bodies, the killing caused an enormous stir in Texas. Governor Jim Ferguson offered a $10,000 reward for Cano, and four troops of cavalry were shifted from Fort Bliss to Alpine, Marfa, Presidio, and Sierra Blanca to look for him. Chico Cano was never caught. He went on to become a figure in the border troubles that grew out of the Mexican Revolution and died in his bed at the age of fifty-six in 1943.

Carry Huffman calls Sitter's and Hulen's murders "the ultimate Cold Case File." No one was ever brought to trial; in fact there is no hard evidence that Chico Cano was involved. Huffman has searched while on patrol for the little canyon where it all happened and thinks he has found it. There may still be evidence there, he says, that could reveal who the murderers were. Until that is found and analyzed, he told me, "In my mind it is an unsolved murder." He may be the man who solves it.

October 11, 2007

✥ 13 ✥

TWO VIEJOS
AT A KITCHEN TABLE

I SPENT A FRIDAY morning a couple of weeks ago doing what I enjoy almost more than anything and don't get to do often enough. I sat at a kitchen table in Marfa with a couple of gentlemen in their eighties drinking coffee and listening to them trade stories. Jack Brunson and Doc Whitman have been friends for more than half a century. They first met in the Border Patrol, which Brunson joined in 1951 and Whitman in 1955. They worked together for nearly twenty-five years, until they both retired on the same day in 1978. They are very different in appearance and manner. Brunson is short and gregarious; Whitman is tall and reserved. Brunson is a seasoned raconteur; Whitman often communicates with a quiet smile. But their common life in the Border Patrol has given them plenty to reminisce about.

When Brunson and Whitman joined the Border Patrol, its agents in the Southwest spent most of their time tracking down aliens who were working here illegally and returning them to Mexico. Agents were not popular with ranchers and others who were dependent on those aliens for cheap labor. Brunson told a story to illustrate the double hazards of his job. He and three other agents had gone to Lajitas to check on some Mexicans who were working in a uranium operation there. When they arrived, they saw the men at the mouth of a cave in the side of a mountain above the spot where the mine was being blasted out. Brunson and two other men scrambled up the mountain toward the cave while the fourth agent, Buck Newsome, stayed on horseback below.

Brunson pulled himself up on a boulder that broke loose and rolled down the mountain, leaving him stranded in a precarious spot. He shouted for help, and Newsome rode up the slope and threw two lariats to the agents above Brunson, who tied them together and pulled Brunson to safety. In the meantime, the mine owner appeared in a pickup truck, driving toward Newsome and yelling at him. Just before he reached Newsome there was an explosion that blew the right front wheel off the truck. The mine owner jumped out of the cab and started cussing at Newsome, wanting to know why the agents were shooting at him. Newsome looked down from his horse and said, "They're not shooting at you; you ran over a dynamite cap." The man stopped in midsentence, looked at the ground, and said, "I've been telling them boys to be more careful with that dynamite."

One of Brunson and Whitman's former colleagues was Bill Jordan, a six-foot-six Louisianan and former Marine who was famous within the Border Patrol for the speed with which he could draw his pistol. Jordan liked to stand facing another agent with his pistol holstered and ask the agent to clap his hands when he saw Jordan start to move. When the agent brought his palms together Jordan's pistol would be between them. Brunson once asked Jordan, "What good does all that fast-draw practice do you?" Jordan answered, "Well, when I go to check out a bar, I know I'm not going to come out a dead man." After Jordan retired from the Border Patrol, he became a field representative for the National Rifle Association, giving fast-draw demonstrations on a number of television programs. He invented a special holster that was used by the Border Patrol as long as they carried revolvers.

Brunson and Whitman agreed that in their days, the Border Patrol had a higher standard of marksmanship than other law-enforcement agencies. "We had to qualify as marksmen with our pistols four times a year," Whitman said. "We carried .38 Specials, most of them Colts." Brunson said he only fired one shot at a person during his career. "And I didn't shoot at him," he emphasized. "I shot near him." Brunson explained that he and his partner had pulled up to a ranch house near Bakersfield and "the bunk house just exploded. My partner took off after a bunch on foot and I was trying to head one off in the car. He jumped into a canyon and ran up the other side, turned around, and gave me an obscene gesture. I had a tremendous sinus headache and I was mad and thought I'd just scare him, so I fired a shot to what I thought was one side of him. The bullet hit the ground right between his feet. He took off running and then he'd stop and vomit and then run some more and stop and vomit again. It cured any desire I ever had to use a pistol. I drew my gun again, but I never fired it."

The men talked about some of the local lawmen they had worked with. Jim Nance, the sheriff in Sanderson, had a high-powered rifle that he was extremely proud of. He liked to demonstrate how it could propel a bullet through a steel rail at close range, until one day the bullet hit the flange of the rail and ricocheted back and winged him. After that he just told people what it could do.

Whitman, who was a master tracker—"I still keep my eye on the ground when I walk," he said—recalled tracking a man who had stolen a rifle from a ranch near Marathon all the way to Black Gap. He was accompanied by Sheriff Jim Skinner of Alpine. "Sheriff Skinner didn't allow hats or caps at his dances," Brunson interjected. "If he had to ask you a second time to take it off, it came off with a blackjack." Whitman recalled asking a couple of young men from Alpine if they knew Sheriff Skinner. "We sure do," they said, putting both hands on top of their heads as if to protect them.

While we were talking, a man knocked on Brunson's door to deliver three beautifully boxed dolls that Brunson had won at a Border Patrol retirees' raffle. "They've been around the office for a month," the man said. "Nobody knew whose they were." "Jack doesn't look like a man who would play with dolls," I put in. "You haven't known him very long," Doc Whitman said with a slow smile.

September 8, 2011

✛ 14 ✛

ALAN TENNANT
AND THE RATTLESNAKES

THERE ARE NO rattlesnakes in England, so when the first English colonists came to North America rattlers made a big impression on them. One of the oldest American ballads is a song called "Springfield Mountain," written in the 1760s about a young man who is fatally bitten by a rattlesnake while mowing a meadow. He staggers to his beloved's house, and she tries to suck the poison out, but it enters a rotten tooth and they both die. The song ends, *Come all you friends, and warning take / Don't never get bit by a rattler snake.*

The other day my neighbor Alan Tennant and I were discussing rattler snakes over lunch at Nel's in Fort Davis. While Tennant did not exactly write the book on rattlesnakes — that was done in 1956 by Laurence Monroe Klauber, whose 1533-page *Rattlesnakes: Their Habits, Life Histories, and Influences on Mankind* is the last word on the subject — his book, *Snakes of Texas*, published in 1984, covers the subject of Texas rattlers pretty thoroughly. There is a good story behind the publication of this book, but Tennant made me promise not to include it here because he's saving it for the book he plans to write himself someday.

There is a good story behind most of the events in Tennant's life, and a conversation with him tends to veer from tale to tale, a little like playing a very fast pinball machine. Tennant is a spring-loaded, wiry, athletic man in his late sixties with green eyes and a clipped black moustache that seems to grow upward from his lip.

Over the years, he has followed a falcon in an airplane from Texas to the Arctic, led birding tours to Africa, swum with sharks in the Gulf of Thailand, and pedaled a bicycle into the Colombian Andes. When I talked with him he had just returned from several weeks of trekking along the border between Myanmar and Thailand, hobnobbing with exiles from Myanmar on the Thai side of the line.

Our conversation about rattlesnakes was provoked by a recent newspaper photograph of a man holding a huge rattler killed near Coleman, Texas. Tennant explained the ways that the size of a dead rattlesnake can be inflated. The simplest, he said, was to hold the body of the snake up close to the camera lens while positioning yourself as far away from the lens as possible, which distorts the size of the snake in relation to your own body. Fishermen learned to do this shortly after cameras were invented. The outsized rattler skins mounted on boards in West Texas bars, he said, were created by wetting and slowly stretching the skin of a normal-sized snake. This technique can be easily detected because it leaves spaces between the scales, which would normally overlap. A less time-consuming way of achieving the same effect is to graft a rattlesnake head and tail onto a python skin, producing the kind of giant reptile that Tennant once saw displayed in a bar in Freer.

We discussed the number of stories about rattlesnakes that we had both heard growing up in Texas, and Tennant reminded me that the ultimate compendium of these stories was J. Frank Dobie's book *Rattlesnakes*, published posthumously in 1965, a year after Dobie's death. Dobie put every story he had ever heard about rattlesnakes into this volume, without vouching for the truth of any of them—he was a folklorist and not a scientist. He tells about rattlers killed that were eight feet long, ten feet long, even eighteen feet long. After recounting these whoppers he says, "The way to make a record at snake-killing is to be off away from tape measures or yardsticks or scales and not to have too many witnesses."

Tennant assured me that the biggest rattlesnakes found in the wild in Texas run about seven feet long. These are in the brush country of the lower Rio Grande Valley, where there is no winter and a snake can eat all year long, achieving a life span of ten to fifteen years. Snakes in captivity can eat more, live longer, and grow larger, Tennant said, adding with a shudder that in some of the less reputable roadside snake farms the reptiles are force fed to increase their size.

We talked about stories concerning the power of the rattler's venom. Tennant said that one of the oldest and most-frequently repeated of these is what he called the "Grandfather's Boot" story. It goes like this: Grandpa is bitten by a rattler out in a field and dies. He is wearing a fine pair of boots at the time, which his widow puts away in a closet after the funeral. Years later, his grandson finds the boots and pulls them on, stands up, and keels over dead, because the fang of the rattler that killed Grandpa is still stuck in the boot and penetrates the boy's heel. Dobie tells an elaborate version of this story, involving a young cowboy who buys a fine pair of handmade boots to court his girl in. He is bitten by a rattler while wearing the boots and dies, leaving the boots to his best friend. The best friend falls in love with the dead man's girl, wears the boots to go courting, and he sickens and dies, leaving the boots to a third cowboy who courts the girl with the same result. The girl is suspected of having some fatal influence until a rattlesnake fang is found in one of the boots. Tennant says that these stories are absolute nonsense because the venom loses its efficacy after only a few hours' exposure to the atmosphere, and the fang is not poisonous in itself, but is only a hollow tube that conducts the venom. Another rattlesnake story that can be dismissed, Tennant says, is that rattlesnakes can be deterred from sharing your bedroll at night by placing a horsehair rope around it before turning in. "Why would a critter that lives in a prickly pear patch be stopped by a little hairy rope?" he asked.

We agreed that one piece of folk advice found in the "Springfield Mountain" ballad was still good, and not just for lovers. One of the verses says *And mind, when you're in love don't pass / Too near to patches of high grass.* That's where the rattlers are.

November 24, 2010

✤ 15 ✤

COLONEL CRIMMINS, THE RATTLESNAKE VENOM MAN

IN JULY 1926 a young man named Jesús Ramirez and a friend were walking down the highway from Asherton, Texas, to Eagle Pass, hoping to find work in the border town. The two men stopped to rest for a minute, and Ramirez was bitten on the arm by a rattlesnake. His companion flagged down a car and they were driven to the Eagle Pass hospital, where Ramirez was given first aid and put to bed. The next morning the Maverick County sheriff, Albert Hausser, was told about the incident and was also told that Ramirez was not expected to live through the day, as a rattlesnake bite in those days was considered to be fatal.

Hausser recalled that he had read about a new rattlesnake-bite serum that was being developed at Fort Sam Houston. He got on the phone, called the *San Antonio Light*, and explained the situation. A few minutes later, he got a telegram from Colonel Martin Crimmins at Fort Sam that read "Major Scott with rattlesnake serum leaves Kelly Field immediately for Eagle Pass." An hour and fifteen minutes later, an army biplane set down in Eagle Pass with the serum and Ramirez's life was saved. The story made every paper in the United States and most of them in Mexico. The Piedras Negras paper carried it with an imaginative drawing of the young man lying in a hospital bed, clutching his arm and looking hopefully out the window at an approaching airplane. The caption below read, "The Airplane That Arrived in Time."

What the newspaper stories did not say was that it was Colonel Martin Crimmins who developed the life-saving serum, by experimenting on himself. Crimmins, who was a frequent visitor to the Big Bend in the 1930s and a much-beloved docent at San Antonio's Witte Museum until his death in 1955, was a professional soldier who first got interested in snakes when he was in Mexico in the Pershing Expedition of 1916. He was stationed for a while in the little town of El Valle, Chihuahua, and to relieve boredom, he started hunting rattlesnakes. He sent two live specimens of a variety he had never seen before to the Museum of Natural History in New York by shipping them in coffee cans. The hard part, Crimmins later said, was persuading the snakes to coil up inside the cans. After he finally got them in, an army photographer came by and wanted a picture of Crimmins holding up the snakes, and he had to shake them out and do it all over again. They were the first live rattlesnake specimens ever received by the museum. They were later classified as *Crotalus lepidus klauberi*, a lethal rattlesnake. Crimmins had collected the specimens barehanded by sticking one in an old sock and tying it to his belt; he put the other in an empty field-glass case he was wearing around his neck.

Crimmins's interest in rattlesnakes continued after he came back from Mexico and was stationed at Camp Bullis, outside of San Antonio. Colonel Harry Henderson recounted to Crimmins's biographer, Chris Emmett, an unforgettable experience: he was once met at the padlocked gate to Camp Bullis by Crimmins, mounted on a magnificent horse and holding a writhing rattlesnake in each hand. "I am Colonel Crimmins," he introduced himself. "I came to bring the keys." He indicated which pocket they were in, and Henderson extracted them while Crimmins held the snakes at arm's length. "I found these two magnificent specimens along the trail," he explained.

Crimmins became interested in developing an antisnakebite serum from snake venom when he learned that an average of five soldiers a year suffered snakebites at Camp Bullis. Doctors in New York and Brazil were experimenting with producing serum by inoculating horses with successively larger doses of snake venom until they became immune, and then using blood drawn from the immune animals to manufacture the serum. After his retirement from the army in 1925, Crimmins became involved in these experiments, some of which included milking venom from live rattlesnakes. This was done by propping the snake's jaws open with a clamp, holding its head over a glass or dish, and repeatedly pressing a gland in its neck, which forces the venom out of the fangs and into the container.

Crimmins was milking rattlesnakes one hot day in Brownsville when the venom in the dish started to congeal. In attempting to pour it into another container while holding a rattlesnake, he managed to swallow a good amount of it, about two hundred drops, he estimated, enough to kill one hundred fifty men if introduced into a blood vein. A hastily-called doctor assured Crimmins that rattlesnake venom ingested directly into the stomach has no ill effects. It does, however, make the person who ingests the venom immune to snakebites, just like the inoculated horses.

A few weeks later Crimmins was at Robert B. Green Hospital in San Antonio when a rattlesnake-bitten baby was brought in who was not expected to live more than an hour. Crimmins persuaded the doctors to give the baby a transfusion of his own blood, and the baby lived for seventy-two hours. At that point Crimmins decided to beef up his immunity, and he got a San Antonio doctor to give him a series of rattlesnake venom injections of increasing strength over a forty-day period. The next time a child was brought to the hospital with a rattlesnake bite and given a transfusion of Crimmins's blood, the child went home the next day. The serum that saved Jesús Ramirez was probably manufactured from Crimmins's own blood.

Martin Crimmins did many other interesting and daring things in his life. He raced dogsleds in Alaska, represented his country at the coronation of the last king of Korea, crossed the

Caucasus in winter in a horse-drawn troika, and shot the rapids of the Rio Grande in Santa Elena Canyon. But nothing that he did required as much courage as allowing a doctor to inject him with rattlesnake venom day after day for forty days, not knowing whether he would live to get the next injection.

October 7, 2010

✤ 16 ✤

TWO GOVERNORS
FOR THE PRICE OF ONE

NOT LONG AGO, my wife
and I were in Austin and
decided to have dinner in the dining room of the Driskill Hotel, an
Austin landmark since its opening in the 1880s. The dining room
is hung with portraits of famous Texans, and when the twenty-
something-year-old hostess directed us to a table under a portrait
of a severe-looking woman wearing rimless glasses and a string of
pearls, I said, "Oh, right under Ma Ferguson." The hostess was
astonished. "How do you know who that is?" she asked. I was astonished in turn. How could any Texan of my generation not recognize a portrait of Miriam Amanda Ferguson? Even though her last
race for governor took place the year that I was born, she and her
husband, Governor James E. "Farmer Jim" Ferguson, were leg-
endary figures of my childhood. Whenever their names came up
in my parents' presence, they would laugh and one of them would
say, "Two governors for the price of one," which was Ma's campaign slogan the first time she was elected governor in 1924. The
Fergusons were a political phenomenon that dominated Texas politics for twenty years, from 1914, when Jim Ferguson was first
elected governor, through 1934, when Miriam Ferguson completed her third term in that office, and the aftereffects of their five
combined terms lasted another twenty years.

Aside from my parents' amused comments, my first brush with
the Fergusons came in my late teens when I started collecting
books about Texas. One of my early acquisitions was a pamphlet
by West Texas journalist Don Biggers, entitled *Our Sacred
Monkeys, or Twenty Years of Jim and Other Jams (Mostly Jim)*, pub-

lished in 1933. I found it in Barber's Book Store in Fort Worth and was attracted by the bizarre title. Over the years I have collected a good deal more Fergusoniana. While I cannot say that I am an admirer of the Fergusons, I will admit to being fascinated by their sustained political effrontery, which I think is unparalleled in Texas history.

Jim Ferguson was certainly not the simple farmer he represented himself to be when he first ran for governor in 1914. He was the president of the First State Bank of Temple, Texas, and a large landowner in Bell County. He seems to have been a Snopes-like individual whose main interest was enriching himself, and he looked upon the governorship as offering wider opportunities for enrichment than a bank presidency in Temple. He put together a coalition of tenant farmers and anti-Prohibitionists and, with a healthy contribution from the brewing industry, defeated his leading opponent, Tom Ball, by forty thousand votes. Ferguson was a demagogue in the same Southern tradition that produced Huey Long, but he lacked Long's ability to produce paved roads and free schoolbooks. What he did have was an extremely combative nature. You were either for him or against him, and his policy was to reward his friends and smite his enemies. By the end of his first term, Texas was divided into Ferguson men and everyone else. He never finished his second term, because those he had smitten caught up with him. He was censured by the legislature, indicted by a Travis County grand jury, and finally impeached and convicted by the legislature. His troubles were brought to a head by his attempt to force the president of the University of Texas to fire four professors who had campaigned against him in 1916, but there was also the matter of state funds which he had shifted to his Temple bank and then neglected to pay interest on. There were nine other charges, most of them dealing with fiscal malfeasance.

In spite of the fact that the terms of his conviction prohibited his ever holding office again in Texas, he ran for governor in 1918 and lost. At about that time he started his own newspaper, the

Ferguson Forum, which Don Biggers described as "a twenty-eight-page paper, containing 3,920 inches of type space, of which 2,674 was advertising and only 1,246 inches was reading matter, if bunk and hot air can be classified as reading matter." The advertising, of course, was a form of political contribution. The *Forum* was given to publishing headlines like, "200,000 LIARS RUNNING LOOSE IN TEXAS!"

In 1920, Ferguson ran for president on his own American Party ticket, losing handily to Warren G. Harding, and in 1922, he was an unsuccessful candidate for the United States Senate. In 1924, he developed a new strategy and ran his wife's successful campaign for governor. Miriam Ferguson was inaugurated just fifteen days after Nellie Tayloe Ross of Wyoming, and became the second woman governor in the history of the United States. Her weaknesses turned out to be granting pardons—she freed an average of two hundred convicts a month—and rumors of cash and land changing hands, and letting fraudulent highway contracts, and in 1926, she was defeated for reelection by Attorney General Dan Moody. But the Depression brought her back into office, and she served two more terms between 1930 and 1934.

Somehow, Ma Ferguson seems a more benign force than Pa, even if she did have a weakness for convicts. In her 1930 inaugural address she invited the people of Texas to "bring their troubles to" her, and they did. I recently had occasion to go through her papers in the Texas State Archives, and they contain hundreds of letters written to her in pencil on cheap tablet paper from Texans who were down on their luck and wanted jobs or money or just sympathy. My favorite was from a woman who wrote that she had taken a train from Dallas to Rusk and the Santa Fe Railroad had lost her suitcase and had promised to send it to her when they found it, but had not done so and could the governor please get her suitcase back? I'll bet no one ever wrote a letter like that to Rick Perry.

August 17, 2006

✥ 17 ✥

PAPPY AND THE
LIGHT CRUST DOUGHBOYS

THE OTHER DAY Michael Baskin, who knows that I like such things, dropped by the house to bring me a campaign card extolling the virtues of W. Lee O'Daniel, a former Texas governor who was running for reelection to the United States Senate when the card was printed in 1942. I was delighted to have it. Not only did it have O'Daniel's portrait, his platform ("The Ten Commandments"), and his motto ("The Golden Rule") on it, it had all of the words to his song "Beautiful Texas" on the back.

Pappy O'Daniel, as he was known, had a miserable record as a Texas governor and US senator, but he played an important role in the history of Texas music. Born in Ohio in 1890, O'Daniel went to work for a Kansas flour-milling company as a stenographer and bookkeeper when he was eighteen. He eventually rose to the position of sales manager. In 1925, he moved to Fort Worth to take a job as sales manager for the Burrus Milling Company. Commercial radio in Texas was in its infancy, and some of the first stations were in Fort Worth. O'Daniel took advantage of the new medium to advertise flour. His success as a radio personality eventually led him into politics, but not until he had established a reputation as an announcer for a series of hillbilly bands that were part of his flour commercials.

The first band that O'Daniel put on the air was a group consisting of Bob Wills, Herman Arnspiger, and Milton Brown. The three men had been playing house parties around Fort Worth as Wills's Fiddle Band, but O'Daniel gave them regular jobs at Burrus Mills at $7.50 a week (Wills drove a truck) and put them on radio station KFJZ as the Light Crust Doughboys, playing an introductory song that went, *Listen everybody from near and far / If you want to know who we are / We're the Light Crust Doughboys from Burrus Mills.* The Doughboys really hit their stride when they went to play at a bakers' convention in Galveston, in 1931. O'Daniel put them on a bus with a rear platform, and they stopped in every county seat between Fort Worth and Galveston, performing from the bus's platform while O'Daniel sold flour between the numbers. By 1934, O'Daniel and the Doughboys were the most popular radio show in the Southwest. They were heard on a network of stations, the Texas Quality Network, in Dallas, Houston, San Antonio, and Oklahoma City. O'Daniel wrote verses which the Doughboys set to music. They included "Beautiful Texas," "Put Me in Your Pocket," and "The Boy Who Never Got Too Big to Comb His Mother's Hair."

Like most bands, the Light Crust Doughboys had a revolving cast. In 1932, Milton Brown left to form his own band, Milton Brown and the Musical Brownies. The next year Bob Wills left to form the Texas Playboys, but the Doughboys continued playing for Burrus Mills until 1942, were revived in the 1950s, and are still around. Country music historian Bill Malone called them "one of the most important parent groups of Texas swing."

O'Daniel broke with Burrus Mills in 1935 and started his own flour company, Hillbilly Flour. The new company had its own radio show and band, the Hillbilly Boys, with vocalists Leon Huff and Kitty Williamson and O'Daniel as announcer. He acquired his nickname, Pappy, from the show's opening line, a woman's voice saying, "Please pass the biscuits, Pappy." He expanded his role on the air to include poetry recitations, Bible readings, and short lectures on morality. Austin lawyer Sam Houston Clinton, a friend of mine in the 1960s, was old enough to remember those broadcasts and could do a hilarious imitation of them, ending each one with, "And now here's some advice for the school children of Texas: Children, always walk on the left-hand side of the road, facing traffic."

The Hillbilly Boys were even more popular on the radio than the Light Crust Doughboys, and in the 1938 election they carried Pappy O'Daniel into the Governor's Mansion. He came in first in a field of thirteen candidates, and while his platform offered no solutions to the problems of the Depression, his campaign certainly took the public's mind off of them. He traveled across the state with the Hillbilly Boys, and his outdoor rallies drew huge crowds. He won the Democratic primary without a runoff and then was re-elected in 1940, becoming the first gubernatorial candidate in Texas history to get more than a million votes.

Once in office O'Daniel proved to be totally inept. He got into a deadlock with the legislature, and no significant legislation was passed during either of his two terms. However, he took good care of his musicians. Every member of the Hillbilly Boys got a state job and one, Jim Byrd, moved his family into a state-owned residence in Austin. The band broadcast a program every Sunday from the front porch of the Governor's Mansion, with the governor as master of ceremonies.

In April 1941, US Senator Morris Sheppard died, and O'Daniel decided to take his place by running in the special June election that would be held to replace him. Texas law required the governor to appoint a temporary senator to fill the vacant seat until the election, and O'Daniel wanted to appoint someone who would not run against him. He selected Sam Houston's last surviving child, eighty-seven-year-old Andrew Jackson Houston. The old man made the trip to Washington, took his Senate seat on June 2, and died on June 20. O'Daniel won the election eight days later.

O'Daniel did not take the Hillbilly Boys to Washington with him, and without them his fellow senators were not as easily impressed by him as the Texas voters had been. He quickly became a nonentity in the Senate, and only won reelection in

1942 by turning to labor baiting, claiming that Communist labor bosses were threatening Texas, which had some of the weakest labor unions in the country. He declined to run again in 1948 after a poll showed that only 7 percent of the voters in Texas would support him.

Pappy O'Daniel was a terrible politician, but deserves to be remembered as one of the fathers of Texas swing and the author of "Beautiful Texas," which in my opinion should be our state song.

April 21, 2010

✤ 18 ✤

THE TWO GARCIAS

TWO TEXANS named Garcia led the fight to end discrimination against Mexican Americans in Texas in the years after World War II. One of them received the Medal of Freedom from President Ronald Reagan and is honored by a nine-foot-high statue in Corpus Christi. The other died an alcoholic in the San Antonio Farmers' Market and has been largely forgotten. Both were men of exceptional ability and courage.

Dr. Hector P. Garcia of Corpus Christi was the founder of the American GI Forum, an organization he started in 1948 to assist Mexican American veterans in their dealings with the Veterans Administration. Just a few months after its founding, Garcia and the GI Forum got involved in an incident that gained them both national prominence and turned the GI Forum into a political force. A funeral home in Three Rivers, Texas, refused to handle the reburial of a GI named Felix Longoria, a native of Three Rivers who had been killed in the Philippines in 1945, and whose remains were being shipped home. Longoria's family felt that the refusal was because Longoria was Mexican, and they called Dr. Garcia. Garcia called Senator Lyndon Johnson, and Johnson arranged for Longoria to be buried in Arlington National Cemetery, with a representative from the White House present. The GI Forum suddenly jumped from being a local veterans' organization to a national political power, with chapters in forty Texas cities as well as in New Mexico and Colorado. After the next few years, under Hector Garcia's leadership, they successfully took on issues such as desegregation of schools and public facilities, poll tax reform, farm labor, and jury selection.

Hector Garcia was born in Llera, Tamaulipas, in 1914, one of seven children of a college professor and a schoolteacher. His parents fled the violence of the Mexican Revolution in 1917 and brought their family to Mercedes, Texas. They encouraged their children to prepare for college; six of the seven eventually received medical degrees. Hector Garcia was the only Mexican American admitted to the University of Texas Medical School in Galveston in 1936. When he finished his residency in 1942, he volunteered for the army and served as an infantry officer before transferring to the medical corps. He was discharged in 1945 and opened a medical practice in Corpus Christi, and it was then that he started trying to assist veterans with their benefits.

Hector Garcia had a remarkable talent for political organization. He was not a rabble-rouser. He was a mild mannered, professorial type, who favored double-breasted suits and striped ties and wore horn-rimmed glasses. But he was methodical and committed, and he always did his homework. He could amass enough evidence and statistics to overwhelm any opponent. He was a supreme strategist, and he led the GI Forum in a series of successful legal battles, culminating in the fight to end the exclusion of Mexican Americans from Texas juries, which went to the Supreme Court in 1954 in the case of *Hernandez v. Texas*. Hector Garcia died in 1996, having received many honors. His statue is in front of the library at Texas A&M Corpus Christi. President Bill Clinton delivered the eulogy at his funeral.

The other Garcia, Gustavo C. Garcia, was the lawyer who represented the GI Forum before the Supreme Court in the Hernandez case. Chief Justice Earl Warren was so impressed with him that he gave him an extra sixteen minutes to present his argument, and the court ruled unanimously in his favor. The decision ended the exclusion of Mexican Americans from Texas juries, which had been a common practice in many counties.

Gus Garcia, as everyone knew him, was a year younger than

Hector Garcia and a very different type of person. He was born in Laredo and raised in San Antonio, where he was a star debater at Thomas Jefferson High School. He went to the University of Texas on an academic scholarship and was captain of the debate team there. He graduated from UT Law School in 1938 with a reputation for brilliance. At the university he befriended future Texas governor John Connally, who was three years behind him. When John and Nellie Connally were married in Austin in 1940, it was Gus Garcia who drove the car that carried the couple away from the church. At the time he was an assistant district attorney in Bexar County, a tall, handsome man with an unruly shock of black hair, a flamboyant courtroom style, and his foot on one of the lower rungs of the ladder that could lead to success in the Texas bar. Maury Maverick Sr. called him "the Mexican John Barrymore."

When the war came, Gus Garcia was drafted into the army, and when he came home after the war he began to use his talents to correct the injustices that Mexican Americans faced in Texas. As an attorney representing the League of United Latin American Citizens and the American GI Forum, he filed a series of lawsuits challenging the Texas system of maintaining separate schools for Mexican American children. These suits came to a head in 1948 in *Delgado v. Bastrop ISD*, in which a federal court ruled that segregation of Mexican American children from other Caucasian students was illegal. Garcia spent the next ten years pressuring local school districts to comply with that ruling, while at the same time serving on the San Antonio School Board and the boards of a wide variety of Mexican American civic organizations. The 1954 Hernandez case was the capstone of his legal career.

After his triumph in the Hernandez case, Gus Garcia's life unraveled. He started drinking heavily, and in 1961 his license to practice law was suspended for two years for writing hot checks. He was in and out of San Antonio hospitals for alcohol-related problems, and when he died of liver failure at forty-eight, he had no permanent address, but was living in the San Antonio Farmers' Market.

There is a glaring error in the Wikipedia article about Gus Garcia. It says that at his death he was penniless and practically friendless. He was penniless, but never friendless. To his last day he could walk into any restaurant on San Antonio's West Side and the diners would stand up and applaud him, honoring him for what he had been.

February 24, 2011

✥ 19 ✥

THE LARK OF THE BORDER

ONE OF MY Christmas gifts from my wife this year was a small *retablo* dedicated to the Mexican American singer Lydia Mendoza. It is a decorated wooden shadow box, painted pink and Virgin Mary blue, surmounted by a cross and containing a tinted photograph of a very young Lydia Mendoza holding a twelve-string guitar. My wife bought it surreptitiously, at Kiowa Gallery in Alpine on one of our visits there last fall, and put it away until Christmas. I was delighted with it because I am a great fan of both Lydia Mendoza's music and Mexican folk art. It is a very appropriate tribute to her artistry, which was directed primarily to the working-class Spanish-speaking people of San Antonio and South Texas. They called her *la alondra de la frontera*, the Lark of the Border, and for fifty years they flocked to see her perform.

The odd thing about my gift is that Lydia Mendoza died five days before Christmas, at the age of ninety-one. I read her obituary on the Internet on Christmas Eve, which made unwrapping her *retablo* the next morning a close-to-supernatural experience. I almost expected to hear her voice singing "El Corrido de Luis Pulido" from the vicinity of the ceiling as I took it out of its box.

Mendoza was born in Houston in 1916, but she spent a good deal of her childhood in her mother's hometown of Monterrey, Nuevo León. Her father worked for the railroad as a locomotive mechanic, and he continually moved his family back and forth between Texas and Mexico. Mendoza first demonstrated her uncanny musical talent as a child in Monterrey. In the 1920s, Mexican chewing gum wrappers had the words of popular songs

printed on them, and Mendoza started collecting them and memorizing the words, although she had no idea what the tunes of the songs were. One day her mother sent her to the corner grocery on an errand, and she discovered that a four-man street orchestra had set up in front of the store. She lingered to listen and quickly realized that they were playing the tunes that she had memorized the words to. Over the next few days she memorized the tunes to all of her gum wrapper songs and then sang them a cappella to her astonished parents. Later in life she bragged to her biographer, Yolanda Broyles-Gonzalez (*Lydia Mendoza's Life in Music,* Oxford University Press, 2001), that she knew the words and tunes to hundreds of songs by heart. Unlike other singers, she never used a songbook or sheet music on stage. She just picked up her twelve-string guitar and sang.

Mendoza learned to play the guitar from her mother, who played and sang at home to entertain her children. Her father also sang, and after he retired from the railroad and settled in San Antonio, he organized a family orchestra that played for tips in barber shops and restaurants, and at food stands in San Antonio's produce market—anywhere that Mexican people gathered. Mendoza remembered that in 1927 they went to the Rio Grande Valley and hitchhiked from town to town, playing for the migrant workers who harvested the Valley's crops. In 1928, they followed the migrant stream to Michigan and played Mexican songs in dance halls there. That same year they made a recording in a San Antonio hotel room for Okeh Records. The Okeh agent asked Mendoza's father what the name of the group was, and he looked around the room and saw a bottle of Carta Blanca beer on a table and said "El Cuarteto Carta Blanca," and that was the name that the family performed under during the 1930s.

Lydia was the mentor of the quartet, even though she was only a teenager. She taught her sister Maria to play the mandolin and the piano, and taught herself to play the violin. She coached her brother Manuel and her sister Juanita in a series of comedy skits. As she told Broyles-Gonzalez, "I was the one who lit the fire." The family performed an hour-and-a-half-long variety show in *carpas* (tent shows), in lodge halls, in theaters where Mexican movies were shown—anywhere they could get an audience. They traveled to New Mexico and California. Eventually, Lydia emerged as the main attraction, a soloist with a twelve-string guitar. She sang on the radio, and then started to make records, and the records made her famous all over the Southwest, and in Mexico, and even in South America. In 1982, the National Endowment for the Arts named her a National Heritage Fellow.

In the mid-1950s she made her first appearance in Mexico City, a two-week booking at the Teatro Iris Esperanza, as part of a larger variety show. When the impresario discovered she intended to do a solo performance he told her that would never do in Mexico; women did not sing by themselves there. He insisted on hiring a mariachi band to back her up. She acquiesced, but after their opening number on the first night the audience started yelling, "Get rid of the band! We want to hear Lydia!" and calling out the names of the songs she had recorded. The mariachi band didn't know any of these songs, so she sang them while they stood silently behind her. At the end of the first week, the impresario decided that there was no point in paying the mariachis, and Mendoza triumphantly finished the second week as a soloist.

As a young woman she had a sweet, pure voice, but as she grew older her voice matured and took on a hard edge and an almost masculine tone. I heard her sing once in the 1960s at a *charreada*, a Mexican rodeo, in San Antonio. She was not part of the paid entertainment, but was standing in front of the concession stand after the show, holding a bottle of beer and belting out a *corrido* to a crowd of a hundred or so admirers who had formed a semicircle around her. You could hear her all over the arena, and you could also see how much fun she was having.

My little Lydia Mendoza *retablo* was made by Joe King Carrasco, whose band has popularized Tex-Mex rock and roll all over the country. No one will ever call Carrasco a lark, but I am proud to have his homage to the Lark of the Border sitting on the windowsill of my study.

January 10, 2008

✦ 20 ✦

ALBERT ALVAREZ,
SECRET HISTORIAN

I SOMETIMES WRITE about the secret history of the Big Bend and the people who have recorded it. By secret history, I mean the history of the Spanish-speaking people of the region, which has been omitted from most published histories of the Big Bend. Albert Alvarez of Pecos is such a secret historian. He has spent his working life as a juvenile probation officer and has never published a book, but he has recorded reams of the secret history.

Alvarez is a short, solid man with a broad face that is crinkled with smile lines. You can tell at once that he instinctively likes people. He was born in Brogado, now part of Balmorhea, in 1945, in the adobe house that his great-grandfather built when he came to Brogado from Julimes, Chihuahua, in the late nineteenth century. Alvarez's grandfather and father were also born in that house, but when Alvarez was about to enter the first grade, his family moved to El Paso, and Alvarez went through public school there, graduating from Bel Air High School. But—and this is the key to understanding his love of history—he spent his summers in Pecos with his widowed grandmother, chopping cotton and digging irrigation ditches. When he was about fourteen, he told me, he started asking his grandmother, who was born in Pilares, Texas, in 1888, questions about her life, and writing the answers down in pencil on brown paper grocery bags. "I asked her about little things," Alvarez said. "'What did you eat? How did you cook it?' I asked her so many questions she used to call me *el pregunton*, the inquisitive one." From his grandmother he moved on to the old men who lived in her neighborhood, men who had been cowboys or farmers or railroad workers. "They took me in and told me their stories," Alvarez said, "and I wrote them down." At some point Alvarez graduated from writing on grocery bags to writing in big bound ledgers, the kind you could buy in five- and ten-cent stores, and he now has a footlocker full of these in his study, along with a file cabinet full of papers and a closet crammed with photographs, records, and notes. He has been talking to Mexican Americans and writing down what they tell him for fifty years.

Alvarez has three essential attributes of a historian: innate curiosity, an ability to get into a conversation with anybody, and an incredible memory for dates. In telling me about his military career (he joined the Marines when he graduated from high school and served two hitches in Vietnam), he mentioned meeting a Vietnam buddy at the Marine base in Quantico, Virginia. "He had been wounded next to me on a patrol on October 24, 1965," he said. A few minutes later, showing me a photograph of his Combined Action Company taken in the jungle in Vietnam, he said, "That was taken on July 3, 1967." Alvarez told me that his stint at Quantico was the best job he had in the Marines. "I was attached to an officer candidate school, where I demonstrated machine-gun fire. An officer would lecture to a class about the different types of fire, and then he would point to me and I would pull the trigger and show them what he was talking about. I didn't have to pick the brass up; I didn't have to clean the weapon; just pull the trigger. I think my finger is still bent," he said, holding up his right hand and grinning.

When Alvarez got out of the Marines he came back to El Paso, married Ester Gallego (a cousin of Pete Gallego), and started looking for a job. He found one at the El Paso County Juvenile Probation Department. "I started there as night janitor, working ten hours six nights a week, and I retired forty years later as chief juvenile probation officer." Alvarez explained that in the early

1980s he left El Paso and came to Pecos as chief probation officer for Reeves County, and then in 2001 returned to El Paso to become chief probation officer there.

It was during his years as probation officer in Pecos that Alvarez started drawing on the material in his notebooks to write an occasional column called *"Recruerdos de Mi Pueblo"* ("Memories of My People") for the *Pecos Enterprise*. He read me one about his experience chopping cotton in Pecos as a boy. It is the best thing I have ever seen in print on the subject. Alvarez describes how the labor contractors' trucks would drive though the Mexican section of town before dawn, picking up the workers; how occasionally someone would shout from a house, "I'm not going today," and the men in the truck would shout back, "You'd better get up, you lazy bastard;" and how they would keep one eye on the weeds in front of them and the other looking out for the *migra*, the Border Patrol, so they could warn the illegal aliens working with them; how on Saturday mornings the contractors would drive around the Mexican section with a shoebox full of cash, paying each worker off at the rate of sixty cents per hour, less a dime per hour for the contractor's commission. The piece is written with telling detail, and it records an experience that was at the core of life for many Texans but that few have troubled to describe.

Alvarez wrote over a hundred columns like this. He told me that several years ago someone at an archive at Princeton University called him and asked if he would send a disc of them to Princeton. "I don't know what you mean by a disc," he told them. "I wrote them in pencil on sheets of paper."

Alvarez is a remarkable man, a close observer, and a fine writer with a sharp sense of humor. His friend, Reeves County Court-at-Law Judge Lee Green, used to tell him that he was the Mexican Mark Twain. His newspaper columns, like Twain's, should be published as a book.

January 26, 2012

✣ 21 ✣

MARY BONKEMEYER
AND THE GRITS TREES

NOT LONG AGO at a party in Marfa, I heard a woman behind me say, in a broad Southern accent, "When I was in college there were some very gullible Northern girls who wanted to know about the South, so I told them that I had grown up on my father's grits plantation, and that every morning my job was to take my bed sheets and spread them under the grits trees and then shake the trees so that we could have fresh grits for breakfast." I turned around to see that the speaker was Mary Bonkemeyer, the mother of Marfa architect Kristin Bonkemeyer, and that she had an impish grin on her face.

A few days later, I sat down with Mary Bonkemeyer at the house of her daughter and son-in-law, Doug Humble, where she is visiting from Santa Fe, New Mexico, while a show of her paintings is up at the Marfa Book Company. Bonkemeyer, who is eighty-seven, has been painting for seventy years, and her work is as fresh and exciting as it must have been in the 1930s. She is pretty fresh, too. "The most wonderful thing you can have as you grow older," she told me, "is curiosity. I keep asking questions and trying to frame questions and work at them while I'm painting. Right now I like to dream about the Golden Ratio."

Bonkemeyer feels that she has always seen things differently from other people. Her father was a Methodist minister in North Carolina, and one of her earliest memories is of disappearing from the parsonage one afternoon to go sit on eggs in the henhouse. "It's my first memory of creating a stir," she said. "When my parents finally found me there was a discussion about whether or not to punish me. I thought I was doing the right thing, helping the hens." In high school she was kicked out of her home economics class for using a rolling pin backwards. "Everything I did in high school was backwards, too," she told me. "I was always being sent out of the class to go do something else while the class was at work. My report cards always said, 'Mary Alice does not follow instructions.' I hated absolutes."

The one thing that she liked was art. "That grabbed my interest," she said. "In the first grade I loved shaping letters. I could get attention from my penmanship." The public schools she attended in North Carolina did not offer art classes, considering them frivolous, but when Bonkemeyer went to Greensboro College (where she impersonated a grits planter's daughter) she had an art teacher who encouraged her and persuaded her to transfer to the University of North Carolina, which, she said, "had a serious art program, but not too serious." From there she went on to graduate school at the University of Iowa, where the painters admired by the faculty were realists like Grant Wood. "I thought Wood's work was too journalistic," Bonkemeyer told me. "I wanted to be a little more Frenchy. I liked Matisse and Picasso and Jackson Pollock. I would unroll a length of newspaper down the hall of my dorm and splash paint on it. I was interested in the accidental and in chaos and how to make sense out of chaos. I was ahead of my time, but somehow my teachers didn't appreciate it."

One teacher who did appreciate Bonkemeyer's work was the pioneer abstract expressionist Philip Guston, who, she said, "taught me how to look at something and transpose the literal into an altered state. I learned that the literal is not necessarily reality. I learned to take something to the very edge. It's like looking over the edge and saying, 'Oooh!' It takes your breath away. An abstraction may be closer to the truth."

In 1940, Bonkemeyer married her college boyfriend, an engineer who was a captain in the army ordinance corps and was stationed in Washington, DC. They lived in Washington for the next thirty-nine years while her husband developed weapons for the army. "During the Vietnam War I told my friends that he was a ski instructor," she said. In Washington, Bonkemeyer's artistic career flourished. She met Duncan Phillips, a wealthy collector of twentieth-century art who established a gallery in his mansion near Dupont Circle. Phillips bought one of her paintings and then invited her to join a group of artists who met to paint in a studio on the top floor of his mansion. "It was heaven," Bonkemeyer said. "Climbing the stairs to the studio I walked by paintings by Braque and Klee and Picasso." The studio could have been an entrée to Washington's upper social circles. Phillips's wife, Marjorie, painted there, and so did Alice Stanley Acheson, whose husband, Dean Acheson, was Harry Truman's secretary of state. But Bonkemeyer, always the individualist, did not take advantage of those contacts. She says, "I was the only one willing to take chances. The others were just trying to impress whoever was there."

Bonkemeyer's husband retired in 1979 and the couple moved to San Miguel Allende. "My goal was to find a climate where we could live without air conditioning," Bonkemeyer told me, "and that led us to Mexico." They lived there for ten years. Bonkemeyer became a faculty member at the Escuela de Bellas Artes, where she says she taught a lot of young Texans. After her husband's death she moved to Santa Fe, where she now has her studio.

I asked Bonkemeyer if her style had changed over seventy years and she said, "No, it has just deepened. I feel that I have finally understood how to create light in painting and how to work with form in a more controlled way, but a painter has to realize that too much control can ruin the creative process. You have to be able to accept the gift of accidents." Then that grin that I had seen at the party appeared, and she added, "In the beginning I didn't like the literal and I still don't." Mary Bonkemeyer is still shaking the grits tree.

April 10, 2008

✤ 22 ✤

GENE MILLER, RANCH WIFE

FOR GENE MILLER, the hardest years of her life as a ranch wife were the years she had to live in town. Gene, who is my neighbor in Fort Davis, grew up as a city girl in Vancouver, British Columbia. She met her husband, Fort Davis cowboy Roe Miller, during World War II. He was a US Navy flier, stationed at Whidbey Island, Washington, and Gene was working for the Canadian general in charge of Canada's Pacific coast war zone. They were married in April 1945, and when Roe got his discharge six months later he brought his Canadian bride home to the trans-Pecos. He took a job as the manager of the Rockpile Division of the Reynolds Cattle Company's Long X Ranch, and the Millers lived in a camp house near the Rockpile. It was an extremely isolated place. The road to Fort Davis was unpaved and the house had no telephone. In fact, when they first moved in, it had no electricity, and the young couple rose and went to bed by kerosene lamps. Nor did it have indoor plumbing. Gene Miller later wrote about those days that "We started out in a house with a path, but soon graduated to a house with a bath." Their water came from a cistern in the Rockpile and was piped into the house by gravity. It is hard to imagine a place more different from urban Vancouver.

Roe Miller worked for the Long X before the war and loved his work. "He always wanted to be horseback," Gene told me. "His life was living horseback." When Pearl Harbor was bombed, he told the Reynolds that he had to join up, but that he would be back when the war was over. His roots were deep in Jeff Davis County. He grew up in his father's apple orchard in Limpia Canyon, where his great-uncle, Victor Moreau Ward, had planted the first trees in

1895. Some of his wartime comrades found new lives in exotic places after the war, but Roe Miller headed straight back to the Davis Mountains and the Long X.

Gene knew what to expect. After their wedding, her husband was given a honeymoon furlough, and he took her to Fort Davis to meet his parents. Their train stopped in Orogrande, New Mexico, at dawn. Miller raised the shade in their Pullman berth and looked out of the window at an endless landscape of sagebrush, rocks, and prickly pear. "It's beginning to look like home," he said. Gene, who grew up among the lush, fog-shrouded forests of British Columbia, cried.

But she quickly learned to love her new home. "Rockpile Ranch was the polar opposite of anything I had ever known," she told me. "Vancouver is not a little town." From the Rockpile it was forty miles to Fort Davis, which was hardly a town at all. But Gene enjoyed being close to nature, and she and Roe, being young and in love, came to treasure the isolation. They kept a milk cow, and Gene churned butter in a hand-cranked churn. "I made hundreds of pounds of it," she said. Eventually, after their house was wired for electricity, Roe's parents gave them an electric churn. She learned to drive a truck and pull a trailer behind it, and she kept chickens, gathered eggs, and fixed windmills. She and Roe had two children—a girl, Sandra, and a boy, Thomas. She thought they lived in paradise.

It was the children who ended Gene's ranch life. Back then, ranch children who were old enough to go to school moved into town. If there was a school bus, it didn't run by the Rockpile. When Sandra was seven, Gene took her and her little brother and moved into Fort Davis, leaving Roe on the ranch by himself. She rented an apartment behind Rita Sproul's boarding house on Court Street and lived in town five days a week, going back to the ranch with the children on Friday afternoon and staying there until Sunday afternoon. Other ranch wives did the same thing. Gene said that her tutor in town life was Margie Grubb, who had four children in school and spent the week at the Grubb family home across the street from the Methodist church. But Gene missed the ranch, and most of all she missed her husband.

In 1956, Roe Miller was offered a job managing a ranch in Montana that was owned by Jeff Davis County rancher Ben Gearhart. The ranch was near Pompey's Pillar, Montana, a tiny community on the Yellowstone River between Billings and Miles City. The ranch was even more isolated than the Rockpile, but it had one great advantage: it was on a school bus route, and the Millers jumped at it. Gene was back on a ranch again, even though she had to drive the children four miles to the bus stop every day, "through snow and ice," she remembers. She took to Montana ranch life with the same zest that she had taken to life at the Rockpile; she adored it. But after they had been there for three years Gearhart sold the ranch, and the Millers moved back to town, this time to Tornillo, Texas, where Roe managed a feedlot and the children went to school in nearby Fabens. They lived near the feedlot, which Gene recalls was "redolent," but they had the consolation of knowing that their children were getting a good education in the Fabens schools.

As soon as Sandra and Thomas graduated from high school, Roe Miller took a job as manager of a ninety-section ranch near Orla, Texas, a wide spot in the road between Pecos and Carlsbad. Roe was back on horseback—"he was horseback every day," Gene recalled—and Gene was back in heaven. "We didn't have to go to town unless we wanted to," she told me. They lived on that ranch sixteen years, until illness forced Roe to retire and they moved into his old family house in Fort Davis. Gene is a widow in her eighties now, but she still has the sparkle in her eye and the zest for life that attracted Roe sixty years ago.

October 19, 2006

✤ 23 ✤

RUSSELL LEE, PHOTOGRAPHER

SOME TIME BACK I wrote about two New Deal agencies, the WPA and the CCC, that left a lasting mark on the Texas landscape. There was a third agency, the Farm Security Administration, that also left a legacy in Texas, but it was a legacy of photographs rather than buildings. The FSA, which was created in 1935 as the Resettlement Administration in order to help tenant farmers acquire their own land, had a Historical Section whose job was to make a photographic record of its work. Its photographers, under the direction of Roy Stryker, created an unparalleled record of American rural life. Nothing like it had been done before or has been done since. Stryker, working from an office in Washington, carefully guided his photographers by sending them lists of subjects to photograph, sometimes even suggesting specific shots. The photographers developed their film in the field and sent the negatives to Washington to be printed; the prints were then returned to the photographers to be captioned and then mailed back to Washington. The most famous FSA photograph is Dorothea Lange's portrait of the migrant mother, but it is just one of 164,000 FSA pictures on file in the Library of Congress.

Among those images are five thousand photographs taken in Texas between 1935 and 1943. Five FSA photographers, including Dorothea Lange, worked in Texas. The one who covered the most miles and took the most pictures was Russell Lee, who in February 1939 was assigned by Stryker to document migrant labor, rural health problems, and farm mechanization, three matters of great concern to the FSA, in Texas. Lee was assisted on his Texas trip by his wife, Jean, who wrote caption notes while Lee was taking pictures, helped develop the film in windowless hotel bathrooms, and kept track of the packages of negatives and prints that went back and forth to Washington.

The Lees spent thirteen months in Texas, zigzagging across the state several times. They photographed migrant cotton pickers in the Rio Grande Valley, pecan shellers in San Antonio, oil field workers in Kilgore, cowboys in Spur, a boot maker in Alpine, turkey pluckers in Brownwood, and stock show attendees in San Angelo. Lee felt that his mission was to show how the Depression was affecting rural people, to portray people who were having a hard time. Rather than make single photos, he shot pictures in series, each series telling a story. He used a Graphic press camera with a flash attachment, which enabled him to photograph people in their homes and workplaces.

Lee's photos have the quality of an eccentric family album. He had an open smile that crinkled his whole face and put his subjects completely at ease. Roy Stryker described traveling with him in Minnesota when he stopped to take a picture of an old lady with a peculiar hairdo. Stryker said Lee chatted with the woman for a few minutes and she invited them both to her house for lunch, invited some friends over to have their pictures taken, and fed them supper, too.

Lee still had that smile when I knew him in Austin in the 1970s. He told me that when he and Jean were taking pictures on the square in San Augustine, Texas, they encountered a man who was familiar with traveling portrait photographers but had never met a photojournalist. "I don't have enough money to have my picture made," the man told Lee, "but I'd like to give you a quarter anyway."

Lee's San Augustine photographs are among the most remarkable of all of his Texas pictures. He and Jean had gone to San Augustine, an East Texas town of about two thousand people, to document hookworm, a disease associated with rural poverty. When they arrived, however, they discovered that hookworm was so controversial that the county nurse had nearly been fired for calling attention to it, and she was reluctant to cooperate with them. Lee told me that they were both worn out from travel and that the hotel in San Augustine served delicious meals, so they decided to stay there for a few days and document the whole town. Lee shot about three hundred photos in San Augustine, making it the best-documented small town in America. One series depicts locals with the tools of their trades—the printer at his linotype, the grocer in his store with brooms hanging from the ceiling above him, the fire chief at the wheel of his fire truck, the sheriff in front of a jail cell. Another series shows the town square on a Saturday, when country people came into town in wagons to shop.

One of Lee's San Augustine photos became an icon of American democracy during World War II. He and Jean attended a public meeting held in the county courthouse to discuss the continuation of WPA roadwork in the county. Lee shot a series of pictures at the meeting and one, a photo of the town's leading citizens tilting their chairs back in the front row of the courtroom, with rows of men visible behind them, was widely circulated by the Office of War Information as an example of American democracy at work. Another photo of that series, shot from a lower angle and showing the segregated courtroom's balcony full of black citizens, was definitely not circulated. Lee liked to use this as an example of the dangers of taking a single photo out of the context of its series. He hated having any of his photographs exhibited singly as art.

Some of Lee's most poignant pictures were shot in Crystal City, where a public health nurse took him into the shacks that made up the *colonias* on the edge of town where the migrant workers lived. His photos show children sleeping three or four to a bed, a woman sweeping a dirt floor while a chicken looks on, a *mano* and *metate*, primitive instruments for grinding corn, in the corner of a kitchen. Happier photos were taken at a cowboy dance in Spur and a stock show in San Angelo. My favorite, which I have a print of on the wall of our kitchen, shows a thin-lipped farm woman dressed in her best coat and hat for the Gonzales County Fair, clutching her purse in front of shelves of canned preserves flanked by signs reading, "Hands Off." I'll bet she invited the Lees home for lunch after Lee took that picture.

January 19, 2012

✥ 24 ✥

BILL LEFTWICH, ARTIST

Last week nearly two hundred of Bill Leftwich's friends gathered at St. Joseph's parish hall in Fort Davis to pay a final tribute to him. Bill, who died in Fort Worth on April 27, was not a Catholic, but the parish hall was the only building in town that could hold the number of people who wanted to be there. One of Bill's paintings showing cattle grazing, with a flat-topped mesa in the background, was on the stage. On a table by the door was a framed photograph of Bill taken about 1948, when he looked a lot like James Dean and when, as his widow Mary Alice said, "He was quiet but he wouldn't take anything from anybody." In his eighties he was slim and ramrod straight, with close-cropped silver hair and a courtly and gentle demeanor. He was an extremely nice man and we will miss him in Fort Davis.

Bill once told me that he knew he wanted to be an artist by the time he was five, and that when he was in the third grade he read Will James's *Smokey the Cow Horse*, and from then on he knew that he wanted to be a Western artist. He was lucky enough to be able to spend a good part of his life doing just that, but it took him a while to get there. He never told me much about his childhood, but I know that his parents came to Texas from Oklahoma when he was very young and moved around a good deal, and that he was around horses a lot as a boy. He did get away from home one summer when he was a teenager, but unlike most teenage boys in Texas during the Depression he did not go to work in the oil fields. He went to San Antonio and studied art with Hugo Pohl, who had a studio and art school in his home on E Street. Pohl was a landscape painter and portrait artist of the old Dusseldorf school, and you can see his careful German lines in Bill's paintings. As one of the speakers at the memorial service said, "You don't need a lot of imagination to enjoy Bill's art. You can tell what you are looking at."

Bill entered Texas A&M in 1940, not to major in art but to work toward a degree in agriculture. His undergraduate career was interrupted by Pearl Harbor, and in January 1942 he left college to join the army. Offered his choice of service branches, he picked the cavalry, thinking that at least he knew something about horses. "I was thinking horses," he told me, "but the army was thinking tanks." He ended up as a tank commander in the 92nd Armored Cavalry Reconnaissance Squadron, and in the winter of 1944-1945 was part of the group that spearheaded the 12th Armored Division's lightning advance across France and southern Germany into Austria. At the end of the war he was in England, part of a unit attached to an officers' training camp near Oxford. He told me that he loved the English countryside. He saw a lot of it because he and a buddy got into the habit of "borrowing" the bicycles that the officers left outside the classrooms and riding out into the country on them. "The first time we did it," he told me, "we realized that we might get into trouble when we tried to return them, so we just left them in a ditch and took a bus back to camp. That worked out pretty well, and over the next few months we really depleted the bicycle supply."

Bill came back to the States, married Mary Alice Atchley of Crystal City in 1947, and promptly went broke ranching. While he was trying to figure out how to keep the bank from taking his pickup truck, a recruiter for the United States-Mexico Joint Aftosa Commission came through, looking for Spanish-speaking cowboys to go to Mexico and vaccinate cattle against hoof-and-mouth disease. They were paying $3,838 a year, which looked pretty good to a guy who couldn't make his truck payments. Bill signed up, and he and Mary Alice and their infant son spent the next three years living in tiny villages in central Mexico while Bill vaccinated unwilling cattle, whose even more unwilling owners had been told that the vaccine would weaken their bulls and make their cows sterile. Most of the time, he worked under the protection of Mexican soldiers who had been assigned to the commission. In the evenings he made pen-and-ink sketches of what he had seen during the day. When he came back to the States, his sketches were published by the University of Texas Press in a book called *The Cow Killers*, with Bill's narratives about the incidents shown in the pictures cast into prose by Fred Gipson, who had just written the best-selling novel *Hound-Dog Man*.

Still, Bill's career as an artist did not take off immediately. He went back to A&M, got a degree in animal husbandry, and took a job as the base agronomist at Holloman Air Force Base in New Mexico, where he somehow got involved in repainting the barracks and had them all painted in pastel shades. While he was in New Mexico he also designed the New Mexico state building at the 1964 New York World's Fair. He heard that Governor Jack Campbell was not happy with the design submitted by the New Mexico Association of Architects, and so he sent one in himself, a round adobe building based on New Mexico's Zia sun symbol. The governor loved it, and it was built at Flushing Meadows. "The New Mexico Architects Association was hopping mad, especially when they found out I was a Texan with an ag degree," Bill told me, "but they were just asleep at the switch."

Bill finally got a chance to become a full-time artist when he was working as the US Soil Conservation Agent in Pecos. The First National Bank of Pecos asked him if he would paint a forty-foot mural on their wall, depicting all of the commercial activities in Pecos. He was so excited that he quit his job before he asked the bank how much they intended to pay him. It turned out that they hadn't planned to pay him anything. "But Billy Sol Estes showed me how to make some money out of it," Bill told me. "He suggested that I go to every business in Pecos, and tell them that for $100 I would paint their product into the mural. I did that, and by the end of the day I had $1,700." That $1,700 gave Bill the confidence he needed to become a full-time artist, and he never looked back.

May 14, 2009

✧ 25 ✧

THE PROPELLER MAN
OF MARFA

WE ALL KNOW that Marfa is a center for the visual arts and that people come from all over the world to see the minimalist installations at the Chinati Foundation. Most of us know that several important films have been shot in Marfa, starting with *Giant* in 1954. Many people are aware that Marfa is a gliding and sail-plane mecca, and that international sail-plan competitions have been held here. Some folks even remember that in the 1920s Marfa was known all over the West as the source of purebred Highland Hereford cattle. But as far as I can tell, not more than a dozen people know that fifty years ago Marfa was famous in the aviation world for the handmade airplane propellers built here by Ray Hegy.

Ray Hegy was a genius, a daredevil, and a fine craftsman, and there is no published biography of him. I have had to piece his story together from scattered newspaper clippings and the memories of the few people left in Marfa who knew him. There were never very many of those, because he was a very private man. I am indebted to Dr. Tom DeKunder of Schertz, Texas, for most of my information about his early life. DeKunder befriended Hegy shortly before Hegy's death in 2000 and sent me a collection of clippings about his career before he moved to Marfa in the late 1940s.

Hegy was born in Wisconsin in 1904, the year after the Wright Brothers made their first flight, and he started out in life as a cabinetmaker. But he got into aviation at the age of twenty-one when he answered an ad for expert cabinetmakers to build wooden airplane propellers at the Hamilton Aero Manufacturing Company in Milwaukee. He made laminated wooden props from birch and white pine for both commercial and military aircraft, as well as mahogany props for navy dirigibles. Years later he remembered that the dirigible props had to be hollowed out by hand to reduce their weight, and were then covered with fabric and painted navy gray.

Hegy got the flying bug himself in 1928, and quit the propeller factory to become a barnstormer, doing stunt flying at carnivals and circuses all across the country. A clipping from a 1930 Hartford, Wisconsin, newspaper includes a photograph of Hegy and his friend Norman Zunker standing in front of a single-engine monoplane that they had just built; a later clipping describes Hegy parachuting from the wingtip of a plane piloted by his brother "before the gaze of thousands" at a Fourth of July celebration. A third clipping, dated March 3, 1939, identifies Hegy as the pilot of a plane from which "the veteran Negro parachute jumper, Suicide Willie Jones" jumped over Chicago's Dixie Airport. Jones's gimmick was that he jumped out of the plane at an altitude of thirty-one thousand feet but did not open his parachute until he had fallen nearly six miles and was one thousand feet above the ground.

The next clipping in DeKunder's file is dated 1944. It shows Hegy in an Army Air Force captain's uniform while he was making aerial photographs of the Amazon River in Brazil from a Grumman Goose, a twin-engine amphibian. After the war he went to work for a San Antonio aerial mapping service, and that was what brought him to Marfa. "I was here on a mapping job," he told an interviewer in 1969. "I liked the people, loved the climate, and after comparing it with winters in Wisconsin, I decided to live in Texas."

Hegy married a Marfa schoolteacher and they bought a house on Texas Street. He built the airplane that made him famous—a tiny red biplane that he called the *Chuparosa*, the hummingbird—in a two-room shop behind that house. Hegy drew the plans for the plane in chalk on the wall of his shop in 1950; the plane was not finished until 1959. It was made largely from parts of other planes and was powered by a 65-horsepower Continental engine, with a propeller built by Hegy. The *Chuparosa* was often described as the world's smallest airplane. It was just the right size for Hegy, who stood about five foot four inches and weighed one hundred twenty pounds at most. Hegy flew the Chuparosa to the Experimental Aircraft Association's annual show in Rockford, Illinois, all through the 1960s. Its propeller was so widely admired that Hegy began to get requests from all over the country for custom-built propellers, and he started making them in his Marfa shop.

Fritz Kahl, whose typewritten memoirs his widow, Georgia Lee, graciously let me examine, estimated that Hegy made four thousand propellers in his shop before his death. He made them from laminated wood, and it took him ten to twelve days to build one, but he always worked on several at a time. He shipped them all over the United States. Kahl painted a vivid picture of Hegy walking down the street to the Marfa bus station with a boxed single-blade propeller, as long as he was tall, over each shoulder.

Kahl knew Hegy pretty well because in the summer of 1961 they were partners in something called Humpback Airlines, which used two Cessna 182s to fly Empire Oil Company seismograph crews from Marfa over the Sierra Vieja to the Rio Grande. Kahl recalled that it was tricky flying because they had to take off from the Marfa Airport at forty-eight hundred feet, climb immediately to seven thousand feet to get over the mountains, and then drop to thirty-four hundred feet to land on a strip that was only sixteen hundred feet long. The strip occupied most of the top of a mesa and was known to the pilots, Hegy and Russ White, as "the carrier." Humpback made six flights a day, three in the morning and three in the evening. The morning flights were beautiful, Kahl remembered, but the evening flights were heart stopping, as the temperatures were over one hundred and there were always crosswinds and unpredictable turbulence over the Sierra Vieja. The turbulence, Kahl said, sounded like a rushing waterfall from within the plane cabins. Kahl described Hegy as "a pilot with ten thousand flying hours, an expert at low speeds, short landings, and flying in turbulence." At that time Hegy was nearly sixty years old.

Hegy's shop is still standing behind his house on Texas Street. Documenting and preserving it would be a worthy project for the Marfa and Presidio County Museum.

June 11, 2009

✢ 26 ✢

SMALL-TOWN JOURNALISTS

THE DEATH in December of former Pecos journalist Oscar Griffin Jr. reminded me once more of the importance of freedom of the press in this country, and the American tradition of small-town newspaper editors and reporters standing up for what is right in the face of community pressure to sit down and shut up.

Oscar Griffin was the city editor of the Pecos, Texas, *Independent and Enterprise*, a semiweekly paper, in 1962. In that town of 12,700 people Billy Sol Estes was "like God," as a Pecos citizen told the *New York Times*, adding, "Anyone opposed to him might just as well pack their bags and leave town." Griffin not only opposed Estes, he wrote four investigative articles about his money-juggling schemes that brought Estes six years in prison and won the *Independent and Enterprise* a Pulitzer Prize for distinguished local reporting. For my younger readers and recent Texans, Estes devised a bizarre method for securing $24 million in bank loans from out-of-state banks, using nonexistent fertilizer storage tanks as collateral. The tanks existed on paper because Estes convinced local farmers to purchase them, sight unseen, on credit, with the understanding that Estes would lease them from the purchaser for their cost plus "a convenience fee." As one farmer told Griffin, "It's like pennies from heaven." After the scheme unraveled, Estes became the best-known Texan in America next to Vice President Lyndon Johnson. The Chad Mitchell Trio recorded a song about him called "The Ides of Texas" that included the verse, *While other kids saved up their nickels and dimes / For jellybeans, liq'rice, and fudge / Well, Billy saved too / And when he had enough / He bought him a federal judge.*

Griffin wrote and published his articles in the face of unrelenting opposition from most of Pecos's businessmen and the other Pecos newspaper, the *Daily News*, which Estes had started the year before in hopes of putting the *Independent and Enterprise* out of business. Instead, after the scandal broke, the *Daily News* went into receivership and the *Independent and Enterprise* is still in business as the *Pecos Enterprise*.

Another fighting Texas editor was Penn Jones Jr., who published the *Midlothian Mirror* in the 1950s and '60s. If Jones is remembered at all today it is because he became obsessed with the Kennedy assassination, convinced that the Warren Report was a cover-up for the Joint Chiefs of Staff and the CIA, and published four books on the subject. But Jones was a dogged fighter for what he believed in long before the assassination. He was the son of sharecroppers who worked his way through college, and when he bought the *Mirror* after his discharge from the army in 1946, he announced that his editorial policy would be "to insult those people who fail to meet the obligations they have inherited along with their citizenship."

Jones once took on the city council of Midlothian, which at that time had a population of 1,100, for paving the streets of the black section of town with gravel that was laced with old nails. He displayed fifty pounds of nails that he had picked up there in his office window. He harassed the school board to such an extent that they refused to admit him to their meetings. He said that they informed him that, "We're closing these meetings to keep things from getting out." Midlothian, which is about twenty miles south of Dallas, was a very conservative town in the 1950s, and Jones became increasingly unpopular. He once told a *Texas Observer* reporter, "I've worked hard for my enemies and I deserve every one of them."

Jones's problems with the school board came to a head in 1962, when he published an editorial criticizing them for sanctioning a compulsory school assembly to hear a speaker representing the right-wing John Birch Society. Jones went to the school board office to suggest that they invite Dallas judge Sarah T. Hughes, a liberal Democrat, to present an opposing point of view. In the course of the discussion the high school principal, Roy Irvin, lost his temper and started pounding the five foot two Jones on the head. That same week the proposed speaker showed up in Jones's office to ask him if he considered himself a loyal American, and a second fight ensued. Three days later the *Mirror's* office was firebombed in the middle of the night. But Jones got a paper out the next week and continued to call 'em as he saw 'em until his death in 1998.

My favorite fighting Texas editor was William Cowper Brann, who published a newspaper called the *Iconoclast* in the then-small town of Waco in the 1890s. The *Iconoclast* was a journal dedicated, Brann said, to combating hypocrisy, and in Waco this brought Brann into immediate conflict with several Waco institutions. One of his targets was the American Protective Association, an anti-Catholic, anti-Semitic secret society with a big Waco following. Brann ridiculed them as the "Aggregation of Pusillanimous Asses" and called the allegations of one of their speakers "blackguard bazoo." Other targets were the Baptist Church and Baylor University, which he described as "a storm center of misinformation." His articles excoriating Baylor became more heated when it was discovered that a young Brazilian woman living in the home of Baylor president Rufus Burleson had been seduced and become pregnant by a relative of Burleson's. On April 1, 1898, Brann was shot in the back on a Waco street by an irate Baylor parent. A fighter to the end, Brann managed to draw his own pistol and kill his assailant before he died.

There is a popular poem called "The Soldier" that frequently appears in shop windows around Veterans Day. It includes a line that says, "It is the soldier, not the reporter, who has given us freedom of the press." Don't believe a word of it. Soldiers may protect freedom of the press, but it was given to us by the Bill of Rights and is kept alive by courageous reporters and editors, and thank God for them.

March 8, 2012

✢ 27 ✢

LEE BENNETT
AND MARFA'S HISTORY

N JAPAN, they declare people with special talents national treasures. If we did that in the Big Bend, my first nominee would be Lee Bennett of Marfa. I first heard of Bennett when I worked for the Texas State Historical Association in the 1960s. The Association ran a program for high school students called the Junior Historians, and the director of that program was Ken Ragsdale, who wrote a couple of very good books about the Big Bend. One day Ragsdale came back to the office from a trip to West Texas and told me about a dynamite lady, as he put it, in Marfa, who he said was going to have the best Junior Historian program in Texas. "You can't believe what she's done," he said. "It's amazing." Well, it has taken me thirty-five years to meet Lee Bennett and to find out exactly what she did, and, as Ragsdale said, it is amazing.

What Bennett did was to teach kids to love history, and not just to love it for itself but to love the excitement of doing history. Most people graduate from high school with a sour taste in their mouths about history because they have had to memorize long lists of names and dates without an inkling of what the Diet of Worms or the Treaty of Brest-Litovsk has to do with them, or why they need to know about them. That is because in the United States we have never decided exactly why we teach history in schools, but that is a subject for another day. When Lee Bennett started teaching American history at Marfa High School in 1956, more or less by accident, she remembered that in her own history courses at

Baylor she had to write research papers. She thought that writing a research paper was an integral part of a class, and so she assigned a research paper to each of her Marfa High School students. By a stroke of genius, she assigned it in lieu of a final and, as she told me the other day, students would rather do anything than take a final, and so her classes became extremely popular.

So far there is nothing very extraordinary about this story. But after a few years of grading research papers, Bennett realized that her students did not know how to distinguish good printed sources from questionable ones, and she was getting papers that cited articles in magazines like *Fate* and *True Detective* along with articles in newspapers at the *Southwestern Historical Quarterly*. The way around this, she decided, was to assign her students topics that would send them to primary sources, to their parents and grandparents and whatever documents and photographs they might have. She asked her students to write the histories of their own families, or the histories of local business enterprises and ranches.

This was the point at which Marfa High School students actually started doing history, and started experiencing the thrill of the chase after evidence, which excites even the most sober academic historian. It was also the point at which Bennett parted ways with the majority of the high school history teachers in America, who are content to have their students memorize names and dates. In 1966, Bennett organized a Junior Historian chapter in Marfa, and in 1968, when Ken Ragsdale first mentioned her to me, her students' papers won every prize offered at the state Junior Historian's convention in Austin. "We were so successful people really didn't like to see us coming," she told me. Over the next few years they took not only papers but plays about their topics to Austin, packing the sets into the back of a pickup truck and, on at least one occasion, into a cattle trailer.

By 1980, when Bennett retired from teaching, her students had produced eight hundred carefully footnoted research papers about the history of Marfa and Presidio County. They are in the Marfa Public Library, under the name Junior Historian Files. The other day Bennett and I sat in the room that houses them, pulling them out of file cabinets and thumbing through them. Many of them are illustrated with photographs and copies of documents. One on the Borunda Café has a menu offering a plate of six tamales, with or without gravy, for thirty cents, bound into it. Also in the file cabinets were by-products of the students' research: photograph albums, store ledgers, dance programs, and other items that interviewees had contributed. One such by-product was the complete negative files of a commercial photographer named Francis Duncan, who worked in Marfa in the 1920s; another was a set of albums put together by a doctor in Shafter during the height of the silver mining days there—photographs of the miners and their families, the only known records of these folks.

The Junior Historian Files are especially important because since 1900 about 60 percent of Marfa's population has been made up of Spanish-speaking families. Some were there before the town was founded, ranching along Alamito Creek; others came as refugees from the violence of the Mexican Revolution; others came from Shafter after the silver mine there closed in 1941. Many of them had children or grandchildren in Bennett's history classes, and the papers that those children wrote are the only records of the history of Hispanic Marfa. No history of Marfa can be written without looking at them.

"The real message in these files," Bennett told me, "is that kids have it in them to create something like this. They can do it." That is true, but it takes someone like Lee Bennett to show them that they can.

May 27, 2004

JACK JACKSON
REWRITES TEXAS HISTORY

HAVE YOU EVER wondered why every Texan over forty knows the details of the Texas Revolution by heart, and can tell you at the drop of a hat about the cannon at Gonzales, the Goliad massacre, Travis and the line in the sand at the Alamo, the Mier prisoners and the drawing of the black beans and the white beans, and the other stories that, if Texas were still an independent republic, would make up our national epic? These are not tales that were passed from generation to generation, because most Texans' ancestors were not here in the 1830s, when these events occurred. These stories owe their wide circulation to a little comic book called *Texas History Movies*, which every seventh grader in Texas got a free copy of, courtesy of the Magnolia Petroleum Company, from 1927 to 1960. Literally millions of copies were distributed.

The book was small, only five by seven inches, and was 128 pages long. The cover of the earlier editions showed a movie screen, with curtains drawn back around it and an enthralled audience sitting in front of it watching the Battle of the Alamo. The title, "Texas History Movies," was at the top, and below the audience were the words, "For Young and Old—Interesting and Instructive." Later editions had a simpler red, white, and blue cover. Each page had eight cartoon panels on it, framing a printed caption in the center. A preface explained the technique: "The pictures themselves tell the story and not the printed captions, which serve in the fashion of cinema subtitles." (Remember that this was in the days of silent movies.) The panels themselves, drawn by cartoonist Jack Patton, were clean and simple but were packed with movement and telling detail. The captions were written by *Dallas Morning News* theater critic John Rosenfield Jr. The remarkable thing about the little booklet is that it was published several years before the first American comic books came on the market.

Texas History Movies had its origins in a daily Texas history comic strip produced by Patton and Rosenfield that first appeared in the *Dallas Morning News* in October 1926. The four-panel strip ran until June 1927, when it was suspended, at the request of history teachers all over the state, until school reopened in the fall. When the final installment appeared in June 1928 Patton and Rosenfield had produced sixteen hundred panels that made a lasting impression on the way Texans perceive their past.

The strength of *Texas History Movies* was that it used slang, colloquialisms, and deliberate anachronisms to humanize people from the past. In one memorable panel depicting Mexican soldiers and Austin colonists fraternizing over a game of horseshoes, a soldier about to toss a horseshoe says, "Watch this ringer, Señor Bill," and the colonist replies, "You're full of prunes, Pedro." One of its weaknesses was that to its authors "Texas history" clearly meant the settlement of Texas by Anglo-Americans and the subsequent revolution against Mexico. Over half of its pages were devoted to the years between 1821 and 1848. Another even worse weakness was that it made use of the racial stereotypes of the 1920s to caricature both African Americans and Hispanics in the cruelest of ways. The drawings and the language, viewed at the beginning of the twenty-first century, are almost unbelievable. As a result, it provided an extremely distorted view of Texas history. As novelist Larry McMurtry has said, its images "stopped two generations of public school students dead in their tracks as far as history is concerned." My friend James Crisp, a Texas historian languishing in exile at North Carolina State University, has written feelingly in his book

Sleuthing the Alamo about his own efforts to liberate himself from the effects of *Texas History Movies* as he has become a professional historian.

In 1960, due partially to growing objections from African American and Hispanic groups, Magnolia Petroleum stopped distributing the booklet to schools and turned the copyright over to the Texas State Historical Association. The Association, with the help of a multiracial advisory group, made a well-intentioned effort to clean up the pictures and the text and get the publication back into the schools. Like many such efforts, this one went awry. The net result was that nearly every panel depicting an African American was eliminated, and caricature was replaced by complete absence. Language was altered beyond necessity, so that the horseshoe pitching colonist's brash "You're full of prunes, Pedro," became an innocuous "I'm all eyes, friend." In a panel depicting an eighteenth-century Spanish governor kicking a cat in fury at receiving bad news, the cat was removed with Wite-Out correcting fluid, leaving the governor with one foot inexplicably in the air. In 1984, the Association proudly reported that one hundred thousand copies of the revised booklet had been distributed to schools and not one complaint had been received, but some of the essential vinegar had gone out of the publication. What was needed was not a sanitized version of the old booklet but a completely new start from different assumptions.

I am happy to say that has now happened. The Texas State Historical Association has just published *New Texas History Movies*, written and drawn by Texas historian-artist Jack Jackson. The handsome little book is only forty-eight pages long, but it covers Texas history from the arrival of the Spanish in the Americas to the 1880s and it has none of the flaws of the old volume. Although the irreverent tone of the original book is retained in the text of the new one, Hispanics, Native Americans, and African Americans are presented as active participants in Texas history, and they are depicted with dignity and humanity. While the old book focused largely on the Texas Revolution, Jackson, who died last summer, devoted the first third of the book to the Spanish and Mexican periods, and the Revolution gets only six pages. This is understandable, as Jackson was not only an accomplished artist who started drawing underground comic books in the 1960s, but a scholar whose books on Spanish and Mexican Texas are considered the definitive word on their subjects. *New Texas History Movies* is a fitting memorial to his genius and it is fun to read, too.

October 21, 2009

✥ 29 ✥

MYRRL MCBRIDE,
PRISONER OF WAR

THIS SATURDAY, April 9, will be the sixty-ninth anniversary of the fall of Bataan. The names of Bataan and the island fortress of Corregidor are fading from memory now, in the same way that the names of the World War I battles of the Meuse-Argonne and Belleau Wood had lost their power by the time my generation came along. As a child growing up in the Philippines, Bataan and Corregidor were very real to me. I could look out of the front windows of our Manila house and see the mountainous peninsula of Bataan and the low island of Corregidor across the bay; the sun set behind them every night. One of the verses of my school song began, *Across the blue Pacific, in the shadow of old Bataan.* I knew about the 1942 battle there in which the American army made its last stand against the Japanese, and about General McArthur leaving Corregidor at night in a PT boat, the subsequent surrender, the Death March, and the Japanese prison camps at Camp O'Donnell and Cabanatuan.

Several Big Bend men were on Bataan and Corregidor. One, Myrrl McBride of Fort Davis, survived the Death March and three and a half years of Japanese captivity to come home and tell about his experiences. The McBride family moved to Fort Davis from Marfa in 1933 and opened a café there. Myrrl McBride graduated from Fort Davis High School and went to Sul Ross for two years before moving to New Mexico to attend the University of New Mexico. He was living in Grants, New Mexico, working to earn tuition, when he was caught by the peacetime draft in March

1941. In a letter to Fort Davis journalist Barry Scobee, published in the *Alpine Avalanche* in May 1941, he described how he and a group of other draftees went to Santa Fe by bus, were sworn in at the National Guard armory there, and then sent by train to Fort Bliss, where he was assigned to the 200th Coast Artillery Regiment.

The 200th Coast Artillery was one of the unluckiest regiments in World War II. It was originally formed as a New Mexico National Guard cavalry regiment after World War I, and a lot of young New Mexico men joined it during the Depression because they could fool around with horses and collect a few dollars a month in drill pay. In January 1941, the regiment was called into Federal service and retrained in anti-aircraft gunnery. That summer, because most of its men were Hispanic New Mexicans who could speak Spanish, it was sent to the Philippine Islands. It was still there when Pearl Harbor was bombed, and it covered the withdrawal of the American and Filipino forces in northern Luzon to the Bataan peninsula. The regiment surrendered to the Japanese when Bataan fell. Of its eighteen hundred men, fewer than half made it back home after the war, and of those a third died within a year of their return.

Myrrl McBride managed to write his parents a letter from Bataan. It was dated February 20, 1942, when his unit was subsisting on half-rations in the jungle and was under constant fire. It was the kind of letter a soldier writes to reassure his parents, breezy and jokey, bragging about the writer's good health and bemoaning the lack of entertainment. By the time it was delivered to his parents in October 1942, McBride had endured the Death March and had escaped from prison camp twice.

McBride later wrote that on the second day of the Death March, in which seventy-five thousand sick and starving American and Filipino soldiers were forced to walk sixty miles in the tropical heat without adequate food or water, he made up his mind that, rather than fall into the zombie-like state that gripped most of his comrades, he would stay alert, observe, and learn things that would enable him to survive. He had already befriended a pygmy Igorot hunter on Bataan who taught him to identify edible plants and stalk wild game. After his second escape from prison camp, he subsisted for several weeks by himself in the mountains of Luzon before he was recaptured. When he was released from prison in Japan at the end of the war, he was fluent in three Japanese dialects and was familiar with Japanese customs.

When McBride was recaptured after his second escape attempt, the Japanese sent him to Bilibid Prison in Manila. He thought he was going to be executed, but instead he and a group of other Americans, evidently picked at random, were shipped to Japan. He and his fellow prisoners were put to work in a machine shop in Osaka, assembling diesel engines. Over the next two and a half years McBride rose to the position of prisoner foreman in the shop, instructing new American prisoners and Korean slave workers in the intricacies of diesel engines. Although he was badly beaten and half starved, he survived and gained the confidence of his captors, who bragged that he was their most talented American prisoner. But they eventually discovered that he was carrying out a methodical program of sabotage, rubbing emery powder into the engines, and in May 1945 he was sent to work in a coal mine on the island of Kyushu. He was still there in August 1945 when Japan surrendered and all American prisoners who had survived were liberated.

In December 1945, Myrrl McBride, still in uniform but wearing the Bronze Star, the Purple Heart with two oak leaf clusters, and the Philippine Liberation medal, came back to Fort Davis and spoke to the Mile High Club about his adventures. The Methodist ladies served dinner, enchiladas with rice. No one knew whether to pass the rice to McBride. "Sure," he said, "please pass me the rice. I still like it. The only trouble was that in Japan I didn't get enough of it." McBride went on to a career as a teacher and administrator in the Albuquerque public schools. He died in 1993.

In Las Cruces, New Mexico, there is a memorial to the soldiers of Bataan and Corregidor. It consists of a life-sized bronze statue of three men on the Death March, supporting each other as they step forward. In front of them is a long strip of concrete with a diminishing number of footprints in it, some made by boots and some made by bare feet. The footprints were made by men who survived the march.

April 7, 2011

✤ 30 ✤

SOME TEXAS CONFEDERATES

THE CIVIL WAR is a watershed event in American history, one that still resonates with us. My generation is the last generation that will have known people who knew people who fought in it. I come from a Southern family. Three of my four great-grandfathers were in the Confederate army and the fourth was on his way from Texas to Virginia at the age of thirteen to join up when he met his brothers on the road coming back. They told him Lee had surrendered and it was all over.

I absorbed a lot of Civil War lore from my father, who, as a boy, liked to hang around Confederate veterans and listen to their stories. He knew both of his Confederate grandfathers. His grandfather Border grew up in Ohio but had Southern sympathies, and when the war started he crossed the Ohio River and enlisted as a private in John Hunt Morgan's Second Kentucky Cavalry. He was on Morgan's thousand-mile long cavalry raid through Indiana and Ohio and ended the war, still a private, as part of the cavalry escort that was with Jefferson Davis when he was captured in Georgia. His grandfather Taylor held a higher rank but had a less adventurous war. He was a captain on the staff of General John Bankhead Magruder (known as "Prince John" for his elegant manners and extravagant uniforms) in Galveston, but he got crosswise with Magruder over the general's dealings on the cotton market and was sent into exile as a recruiting officer in his hometown of McKinney, Texas, where for the rest of his life he was Captain Taylor.

Most Texans had a Civil War experience far closer to Captain

Taylor's than to Private Border's. About one hundred thousand Texas men and boys joined the Confederate Army, but two-thirds of them never left the Southwest. They spent the war guarding the borders of Texas against Indians and Yankees or participating in the expansionist schemes of the Confederacy into New Mexico. The ones who did get to the East gave a good account of themselves. Hood's Texas Brigade, four thousand men commanded by General John Bell Hood who lost an arm and a leg leading them, was part of Robert E. Lee's Army of Northern Virginia and fought in twenty-four major battles. By the end of the war the brigade had been reduced to six hundred officers and men. Terry's Texas Rangers, a cavalry brigade raised in Fort Bend and Wharton counties, was on its way to Virginia when it was diverted to Braxton Bragg's Army of Tennessee. Bragg used them as shock troops and they fought with distinction at Shiloh, Murfreesboro, Chickamauga, and in the Atlanta Campaign.

Texas contributed one distinguished general and a number of not-so-distinguished ones to the Confederate Army. John Bell Hood was actually born in Kentucky, but he was serving in Texas with the Second United States Cavalry when the war started and was so disgusted with his native state's failure to leave the Union that he declared himself a Texan. Hood was a natural leader. He stood six feet two and was rawboned and narrow faced, with hair and a beard that was such a light brown that it was almost yellow. His men loved him and would follow him anywhere. He was at his best in battle; he instinctively knew where to direct his blows. Stephen Vincent Benet described him as "all lion, none of the fox." There is a monument to him and his brigade on the state capitol grounds.

War brings fools and hotheads as well as heroes to the fore, and Texas had its share of those, too. Louis T. Wigfall was a combative state legislator from Marshall who got himself elected to the US Senate in 1859 on a proslavery, anti-abolitionist ticket. After

Lincoln's election Wigfall used the Senate floor to urge the slave states to secede, and when Fort Sumter was fired upon he took it upon himself to row out to the fort in a rowboat, wearing civilian clothes but waving a sword, and demand its surrender. The Union officer who pulled him through the casemate found him an astonishing figure. When it came to actual fighting, Wigfall preferred to be elsewhere. After a brief stint as an officer in Hood's Brigade, he ran for the Confederate Congress and spent the next four years harassing Jefferson Davis about his conduct of the war. When it was over Wigfall went to England and tried to foment a war between that country and the United States, hoping that such a war would give the defeated Confederacy a second chance. Wigfall had a loose grip on reality.

John Robert Baylor had no trouble fighting. His problem was that he didn't know when to stop. Baylor was an Indian fighter and Indian hater who, like many early Texans, first came here fleeing a murder charge. In the late 1850s, he edited a newspaper in Weatherford called the *White Man,* in which he urged the extermination of the Comanches. When the war started he became colonel of the Texas Mounted Rifles and led them into New Mexico, where he occupied the town of Mesilla and declared it the capital of the Confederate Territory of Arizona. From Mesilla he and his men led a campaign against the Apaches that was so brutal that other officers complained to the Confederate War Department. Jefferson Davis wrote Baylor a letter telling him to tone it down. In reply Baylor sent the fastidious Davis a blonde woman's scalp, saying he had taken it from an Apache chief he had killed. Davis removed him from military and civil office, wisely deciding that he was no credit to the Confederacy.

Even though this year is the one hundred and fiftieth anniversary of its beginning, the Civil War is nothing to celebrate. It was an American tragedy, leaving six hundred thousand young men dead and a generation of women grieving for them. It might have been avoided, had there been statesmen in Washington who were willing to compromise, rather than fire-eating ideologues on both sides. The Civil War has relevance today. Its commemoration this year should remind us that compromise is the essence of good politics, and the memory of it should show us what awful things can happen when politicians adhere to immovable positions for ideological reasons.

July 7, 2011

✤ 31 ✤

THE JACKSONS OF BLUE
AND OTHER TEXAS CHAIRMAKERS

BACK WHEN I watched television my favorite program was
Antiques Roadshow. It gave me a delicious sense of *Schaden-
freude*—pleasure in the misfortunes of others—when the apprais-
er, a suave, supercilious Sotheby's type, would say to some grand-
motherly lady who had brought in an old cane-bottomed chair,
"Well, Madam, had you not stripped the paint off of that fine
example of a Baltimore side chair made by Thomas Renshaw in
1810 it would be worth $200,000, but as it is I don't think you
could get more than a few dollars for it."

One thing that I never saw brought before the camera on
Antiques Roadshow was an old Texas ladder-back hide-bottom
chair, the kind that were called "common chairs" in the nineteenth century and that sold for $1 apiece for seventy years or so,
escalating up to $2.50 in the 1920s and '30s. You can still pick
them up for $40 or $50 if you know where to look. The only heir-
loom I own is one of these chairs, made for a great-grandmother in
Fannin County, Texas, in the 1840s. It is a particularly handsome
example, made of hickory with a seat of laced rawhide strips, and
it is a fine ornament to our hallway in Fort Davis. No one is
allowed to sit on it.

Chairs like it were made by the hundreds of thousands all over
the South from the 1820s through the 1940s. They were at home
in both log cabins and mansions; Sam Houston had fourteen of
them in the governor's mansion in Austin, according to an inventory taken in 1861. Many of them now in museums and private
collections show wear on the feet of the two back legs from being

tilted back at a comfortable angle, probably against a wall on a front porch during long evenings of story telling, or in front of a pot-bellied stove in a country store.

These chairs were made by artisans called chairmakers, who were distinguished from cabinetmakers because they were less skilled and required fewer tools. In fact, most respectable people considered chairmakers somewhat marginal and looked down on them as not being totally respectable. This attitude probably originated in England, where chairmakers lived in the woods, close to their raw materials, and did not farm or mix much with ordinary folk. In England chairmakers are called bodgers. Folklorist Geraint Jenkins once asked an informant where the word came from, and the answer was, "Because they be always bodgin' about in the woods."

Both English and American chairmakers worked with a minimum toolkit: an axe, a draw knife, a foot-powered lathe, and an auger. They cut their wood in the winter, shaping it into square pieces of the desired lengths with the draw knife and then turning those pieces on the lathe until they had become the posts, legs, and stretchers that made up the chair frame. The flat slats of the ladder back were boiled in water and then pegged to a form to give them a slight curvature. The various parts could then be assembled into chairs and the bottoms stretched over the seat rounds on demand. Some chairmakers took extra care and added little shaped finials to the tops of the back posts, or smoothed them flat above the seat, or scored lines around them to leave a personal signature. Others just slapped the pieces together and that was that.

In Texas, chairmaking tended to run in families. The Dorrises in Caldwell County are a good example. They started making chairs in Tennessee; by the 1850s they had made their way to Texas, and Anderson Dorris and his son had set up a chair factory in Lockhart. They advertised in 1869 that they made "the best article of hide-bottomed chairs," and that for a small additional cost they would substitute a shuck bottom, a bottom made of twisted corn shucks. Eventually eight other Dorrises, all chairmakers, spread out from Lockhart across East Texas and set up shops.

Several years ago Texas antique dealers began turning up hide-bottomed chairs they called "Jackson Blues." These were all made in the community of Blue, in Lee County, by a family named Jackson. No one knows exactly when William Jackson came to Blue and started making chairs, but it was sometime before 1900. The soil around Blue is too sandy to raise much except watermelons, and Jackson must have figured that chairs would be a more profitable enterprise than watermelons. He made them with octagonal back posts, and his sons Andrew and Fayette and his grandsons Harvey, Newell, Oran, and Arman, made them the same way, so they are easily identifiable. Over the years the Jacksons made thousands of chairs. In the 1920s they would pile a load on a Model T truck and drive around the countryside selling chairs. According to some folks they also made whiskey, and after selling a load of chairs they would go back to Blue and stay drunk until they needed money, and then they would hit the road with another load of chairs. Hugh Jackson, a great-grandson of William, made the last Jackson chair in 1970 and sold it for $50.

Over the years I have accumulated several hide-bottom chairs to keep my great-grandmother's chair company. One has a handsome black and white Holstein hide seat, put on by a neighbor in Round Top who made a specialty of rebottoming old chairs. My favorite, though, has a drawer built under the seat. I bought it in Beaumont, and the man who sold it to me explained that it had belonged to a pipe smoker, who added the drawer to hold his pipes and tobacco. It has the telltale tilt-back wear on the back legs, and I imagine its owner enjoyed many pipes of tobacco leaning against a porch wall.

Some people consider a .45 Colt revolver the ultimate frontier artifact, but I'll take a well-worn hide-bottom chair any day.

December 9, 2010

✣ 32 ✣

A BUNCH OF COWBOYS TRYING
TO BUILD AN AIRPLANE

I HAD A VISIT the other day from Lionel Sosa of San Antonio and his wife, Kathy. Sosa is a highly successful businessman, a partner in the largest Hispanic advertising agency in the United States, a consultant to presidential candidates, and an accomplished portrait artist. But that is not what this column is about. This column is about the Lionel Sosa I knew when we were both in our twenties and both working for a loony organization called The San Antonio World's Fair, Inc., better known as HemisFair 68, and about some of the people we both worked with there.

World's fairs are held every three or four years, and they bring a floating population of specialists together with a group of managers who usually have had absolutely no experience in producing a world's fair. The specialists are creative types who often move from fair to fair; the managers are hardheaded businessmen who are determined to make their particular fair the first one in history to show a profit on closing day. Add a group of showmen who produce the fair's entertainment, and you have a highly unstable mixture of deeply interesting people. Someone said that watching HemisFair 68 take shape was like watching a bunch of cowboys trying to build an airplane. But since HemisFair was the only licensed world's fair ever held in Texas, I think it is worth recording something about it.

My job title at the fair was Theme Development Writer. Every licensed world's fair has a theme, assigned by the Bureau of International Expositions in Geneva, and all of the fair's exhibits must address that theme. HemisFair's theme was "The Confluence of Civilizations in the Americas," and my job was to write proposals for commercial exhibits that would fit that theme. Here is how it worked: the sales department would decide to approach the Goodyear Tire Company to buy exhibit space at the fair. They would come to me and say, "We want a proposal for a six thousand square-foot exhibit for Goodyear Tires." I would sit down and write an eight-page concept statement about the history of rubber in the Americas; how the Mayas discovered it; how the Aztecs used it in their ceremonial ballgame, etc. The sales department would take it to Goodyear and Goodyear would say, "Fellows, we're not selling Aztecs, we're selling tires. We want an exhibit with tires in it." I would then have to rework the concept statement to get tires into it. It was a highly frustrating job.

The best part of the fair was the people that I met there. Bill Brammer, author of *The Gay Place*, had an office just down the hall from mine. Brammer was a witty fellow who regularly received packages containing bricks of hashish at his office address, sent through an embassy diplomatic pouch direct from Morocco. At one point someone in the fair's public relations office circulated a list of adjectives to be used in press releases describing the fair. Brammer drew up a counter list, which I wish I had kept because it would be a priceless piece of Texas literary ephemera. The only word I can remember that was on it was "dithyrambic."

Our office got a lot of visitors, some of them clearly unbalanced, with schemes for promoting the fair, and Brammer and Hugh Lowe, another staff member, and I worked out a routine for dealing with them. Brammer would listen to them for half an hour and then say, "You need to see Mr. Lowe," and take them to Lowe's office. Lowe would listen to them for fifteen minutes and say, "You need to see Mr. Taylor," and escort them to my office. I would listen to them for ten minutes and say, "Let's talk about this more over lunch," and take them down the street to the Nueva Street Café, buy them lunch, and then suddenly remember that I had an appointment and leave them over their enchiladas. One gentleman I remember in particular had a trained dog act and wanted the fair to hire him to take his dogs to Broadway openings, where they would walk in circles in front of the theaters on their hind legs, holding little signs in their paws that said, "Visit HemisFair 68." When I left the restaurant he was happily telling the people at the next table about his dogs.

There were a lot of Californians who came to work for the fair. Sosa and I both had fond memories of a graphic designer named Richard Wilson, who was a flower child from San Francisco and infused outlandish colors into the fair's advertising. Wilson was the quintessential Californian, happy to greet anyone with a smile. He liked to explore the back roads of the Hill Country in his Toyota FJ40 jeep. On one occasion when I was with him we were crossing a ranch on a one-lane dirt road, carefully closing unlocked gates behind us, when we saw a pickup truck coming towards us with the driver signaling us to stop. Wilson braked the Toyota, glanced at the door of the pickup, which had lettering on it that said "FJ Hereford Ranch, Boerne, Texas," and jumped out of the Toyota with his hand extended and a big smile on his face, saying, "How ya' doin', Mr. Hereford?" The driver gave us a long look and said, "You boys aren't from around here, are you?"

As the opening date, April 6, drew near, the fair offices took on the atmosphere of a Broadway show about to open. But the summer of 1968 was not a propitious time for a world's fair. Martin Luther King Jr. was assassinated two days before the opening, and riots broke out all over the country; Robert Kennedy was killed eight weeks later. The anticipated crowds did not show up and the fair ended up in the red. But it has paid off a hundredfold since. The new hotels that were built for it, the improvements and extensions of the River Walk, and the energy that it generated changed San Antonio forever and made it Texas's major convention city and tourist destination. Before the fair, the joke was that when Santa

Anna left San Antonio after the Alamo, he said, "Don't do anything until I get back," and no one did. No one can ever say that about San Antonio again.

April 19, 2012

✤ 33 ✤

AMON CARTER AND FORT WORTH

ARECENT VISIT TO Fort Worth made me realize once again how much I love that city, my father's hometown and mine, too. Much of what I love about Fort Worth has to do with Amon Carter. On this trip we visited one of his legacies, the Amon Carter Museum of American Art, dedicated in 1961, six years after his death. When you leave the museum and stand on its portico you see on your right the Will Rogers Memorial Coliseum, built by Carter in 1936 to honor his deceased friend Will Rogers. If you look carefully you can see the equestrian statue of Rogers by Electra Waggoner Biggs, commissioned by Carter. And directly in front of you is the skyline of downtown Fort Worth, which many people would say was also built by Carter. In fact, Broadway producer Billy Rose once told Carter, "I envy you. I build shows, but, Christ, you built a city!"

Amon Carter was the owner and publisher of the *Fort Worth Star-Telegram* from 1908 until his death in 1955 and was Mr. Fort Worth for most of those years. People either loved him or hated him. My grandmother Taylor was in the first category. She thought that Will Stripling, who gave her a job selling china in his Fort Worth department store when she was suddenly widowed in 1922, hung the moon, but she would tell you that Amon Carter lit it up and made it shine.

Carter came to Fort Worth as a brash young man in 1905. He went to work as the advertising manager of the *Fort Worth Star*, and within three years he had bought the paper and merged it with another, creating the *Star-Telegram*. From then on he tirelessly promoted Fort Worth. Although he was a farm boy from East Texas, he took on the persona of a cowboy, wearing enormous Tom Mix-style hats with his business suits and frequently carrying a pair of loaded pistols, which he tended to fire off if he thought things were dull. He liked to climb onto chairs in places like the restaurant of the Mayflower Hotel in Washington, DC, and shout, "Hooray for Fort Worth and West Texas!" He disliked silence, and he could not stand not being the center of attention, wherever he was. Some people found this offensive.

Governor Miriam "Ma" Ferguson was one of those people. She and Carter got into a public donnybrook after Carter paraded behind the gubernatorial box at the 1925 Texas A&M-University of Texas Thanksgiving football game in College Station, shouting "Hooray for Dan Moody and the Texas Aggies!" Dan Moody, the Texas attorney general, had just completed an investigation of corruption in the Ferguson-controlled Texas Highway Department and announced that he would oppose Mrs. Ferguson for governor in the 1926 election, and the *Star-Telegram* was firmly behind Moody. Mrs. Ferguson had a Texas Ranger escort Carter out of the stadium. The incident made the papers all over the country, and Mrs. Ferguson held a press conference in Austin at which she claimed Carter had been drunk and was waving a cane filled with liquor while he was shouting. She then went on to elaborate on Carter's habits, alleging that he bought these canes in wholesale lots to give to his friends, and that he also gave them liquor-filled flasks shaped like family Bibles.

Not able to leave the matter alone, Mrs. Ferguson then wrote a letter to Carter which she sent to every major newspaper in Texas, telling him that she forgave his "apparent discourtesy" to her because she knew that he "was not responsible at the time," and then going on to chastise him for his habits, saying that she knew that he kept a building on the grounds of his home "fitted up in the old fashioned bar room way" where he served "invigorating concoctions" to his guests and gave them "souvenir canes that contained at least one pint of beverage." She concluded by demanding that Carter resign as chairman of the board of the newly-created Texas Technological College, saying that he "displayed vices that are repugnant to strict ideals of morality and sobriety."

Carter replied with his own letter, refusing to resign from anything, denying that he was drunk at the football game, and saying that the governor only accused him of drunkenness because she thought that anyone who supported Dan Moody must be either drunk or crazy. Privately he started referring to the liquor-filled canes, which he indeed gave away at parties, as his "Dan Moody walking canes."

There are hundreds of stories about Amon Carter. He maintained a twenty-year-long feud with Dallas, always taking his lunch along in a paper sack when he had to go there because he refused to spend money on lunch in Dallas. He gave Western hats away to every distinguished visitor to Fort Worth, a special model made up by Stetson called the Shady Oaks, after his estate on the edge of town. He kept Bascom Timmons, head of the *Star-Telegram's* Washington bureau, busy ascertaining the hat sizes of every dignitary who might possibly visit Fort Worth, from Franklin Roosevelt on down. He gave such extravagant parties at Shady Oaks that Elsa Maxwell, queen of Washington party givers, wrote in the guestbook there, *I thought that I would never see / A better host than what I'd be / But Elsa Maxwell's just a starter / When it comes to Amon Carter.*

Above all, Amon Carter set a high standard for eccentricity and made it socially acceptable in Fort Worth to be eccentric. On our recent visit there, my wife and I had an early breakfast at the Ol' South Pancake House on University Drive. A short, pudgy gentleman with curly gray hair, wearing a rancher's vest and cowboy boots, sat at the next table, obviously waiting for someone. At one point he got up and walked outside, and when he came back the waitress said, "Where'd you go?" "I didn't go nowhere," he replied. "I was just walking around barking." Then he cupped his hands over his nose and mouth and barked twice, two short yelps, like a Chihuahua. Amon Carter would have been proud of him.

June 14, 2012

II. TEXAS PLACES

✤ 34 ✤

DARK CORNER AND HIGH HILL

I PROBABLY OWE my affection for country cemeteries to my grandmother Taylor, who could not pass one without stopping. When I was a small boy she would take me on drives in her Studebaker Commander along the country roads around Fort Worth, and whenever a cemetery would come in view she would say, "Let's just stop and see who's in there." As near as I can remember she never knew any of the occupants. She just liked to tut over the dead babies and admire the irises and roses on the graves.

As I grew older, the flora in country cemeteries was their main attraction for me. I came to regard them as miniature nature preserves, set aside by their wroughtiron fences as repositories of plants that had vanished from the surrounding countryside and been superseded by showier hybrid varieties in urban gardens. They were the last refuge of nineteenth-century varieties of daffodils, irises, crepe myrtles, pomegranates, fig trees, and rose bushes, plants that had been brought to Texas farmsteads by settlers from further east and then lovingly transplanted from dooryard to graveyard. For a while, when I lived in the country in Fayette County, I was associated with a group of naturalists called the Brenham Rose Rustlers, who scoured old cemeteries for examples of nineteenth century roses, and I had a magnificent Duchesse de Brabant growing in my own dooryard, rooted from a slip taken from a bush in a cemetery near Frelsburg.

Many of the cemeteries that the Rose Rustlers rustled from were what my friend Anders Saustrup called "geb and gest cemeteries," from the fact that most of the birth and death dates on the tombstones in them were preceded by the abbreviations *geb.* and *gest.*, signifying the German words *geboren*, born, and *gestorben*, died. This was an area that had been settled by German immigrants in the 1840s and '50s, and there always seemed to me to be a special poignancy about the grave of someone who had been born in a German dukedom or principality and had died in Texas, so far from home.

I knew a lady there, a wealthy Houstonian, who bought a country place near La Grange. She liked old cemeteries and thought her place should have one, but the previous owners had neglected to bury anyone there. She was an observant person and she noticed that many of the cemeteries in the area had a mixture of older marble and limestone tombstones and newer red granite markers, but that the death dates on the granite markers were often in the nineteenth century. She inquired around and learned that Sonny Stoltz, the stonecutter in La Grange, had gone around the countryside in the 1950s urging families to replace their old grave markers with modern granite ones, and that he had a big pile of old markers that he had replaced behind his shop. She bought a dozen of them and had Sonny set them up for her. She added some lengths of iron fence and bingo; her place had an old family cemetery on it. Someday it will drive a team of archaeologists crazy—the cult of the missing corpses.

I prefer my cemeteries to be real. Not long ago my wife and I were driving back to Fort Davis from Denton on a series of backroads. Somewhere between Jacksboro and Graham we passed a sign pointing down a dirt road that read "Dark Corner Cemetery." That's my kind of graveyard. Over the years I've encountered other cemeteries with memorable names. There is Lonesome Dove Cemetery in Tarrant County, inspired, I think, not by Larry McMurtry's novel or the television series but by the dove that Noah sent out from the ark. Over in East Texas there is Little Hope

Cemetery, possibly a comment on the heavenly aspirations of its residents. Near Austin there is a Nameless Cemetery, which serves a community also called Nameless, due to the inability of its first settlers to agree on a name.

Between 1880 and 1920 the sentimental rhymed epitaph was very much in fashion, and tombstone cutters had books of these verses in their workshops. The Lanham Mill Cemetery in Somervell County, southwest of Fort Worth and a favorite stopping place of my grandmother's, is chock-full of these. I once copied down a few in a notebook. One reads, *A loved one from us is gone / A voice we loved is stilled / A place is vacant in our home / Which never can be filled.* Another is *Weep not oh! Weep not kindred dear / For her whose last remains lie here / For Jesus she on earth did love / And now she dwells with him above.* An infant's marker bears the inscription, "Sleep on sweet babe and take they rest/ God called thee home he thought it best." Over in the next county, at Acton, the inscriptions are more laconic. I recorded one there that simply read, "Well, I must go home." A finger pointing skyward over the words indicated where home was. The lingering presence of a loved one who has died is nowhere more vividly captured than on a stone at the Macedonia Cemetery in Brazos County: "He is just around the corner a little out of sight."

Sometimes temporary grave decorations carry sentiments, too. The funeral home in Brenham used to supply mourning families with a floral decoration to be set up at the graveside during the funeral that included a red plastic telephone, the old-fashioned kind with a dial, and the words "Jesus Called" spelled out around it in plastic flowers affixed to a Styrofoam backing.

Austin raconteur Frank Oltorff used to tell about the Sunday afternoon walks his Uncle Tom Bartlett would take his children and nieces and nephews on through Calvary Cemetery in their hometown of Marlin, stopping at each grave and commenting on the history of its occupant. One concrete headstone was cast in the shape of an electric light pole to commemorate a man who had met his death while replacing a faulty wire for the local utility company. Bartlett always said that this was a dangerous precedent, opening the way for a series of markers in the shape of phallic symbols and whiskey bottles. I never encountered any electric poles in my cemetery explorations, but I have found tombstones that had references to the deceased's occupation on them. At High Hill in Fayette County several stones are ornamented with carpenter's planes, chisels, hammers, and, in one case, a blacksmith's anvil. There is an extreme example in the cemetery at Seymour, where a rancher named W. H. Portwood is commemorated in a large marble bas-relief that depicts him approaching the Pearly Gates on horseback, leading a pack mule, with Saint Peter standing nearby extending a welcoming hand. Portwood was a wealthy man, and the inclusion of the pack mule is an indication that he intended to take at least some of it with him. The last word, however, is in the Florida Chapel Cemetery at Round Top, where the headstone of a schoolteacher who was known for her loquacity bears the inscription, "She finally stopped talking."

January 27, 2005

✣ 35 ✣

COUNTY COURTHOUSES

PROBABLY because I grew up in Fort Worth, county court-houses have always fascinated me. In fact, I will admit to being a courthouse freak; I will drive miles out of the way to see a really good courthouse. Fort Worth does not have just a good court-house; it has a superb one, a vast red granite pile topped by a two hundred-foot clock tower, which when I was in high school was topped in turn by a metal-and-neon American flag. The court-house sits on a bluff above the Trinity River at the head of Main Street, and it dominates that street even from the railroad station fourteen blocks away. For more than half a century it said to arriv-ing passengers, "You are stepping off the train in no mean city." When my father was in high school a human fly advertising a soft drink called Satanet spent a Saturday afternoon climbing the clock tower while a crowd of several thousand people held their collective breath in the street below. I have never been able to look at the building without seeing that figure clinging to the tower, dressed, as my father recalled, in a red devil suit.

The Fort Worth courthouse was built in 1895 and is a fine example of what courthouse aficionados call the Golden Age of Texas courthouse architecture: ornate, richly embellished, and expensive (it cost $420,000, which was a small fortune in 1895). The first Texas courthouses, back in the days of the Republic, were log cabins or, sometimes, just big trees like the one Judge Robert McAlpin (Three-Legged Willie) Williamson held court under in Columbus in 1837. Log cabin courthouses had certain flaws. Texas courthouse artist Bill Morgan likes to tell about the first log Cooke County courthouse at Gainesville, which was built in 1850 and lasted only three years. It was destroyed when a bull belonging to a local man called Jim Dickson broke out of his nearby pen and charged through the open front door, slamming into the opposite wall and bringing the whole structure down around him like so many toothpicks. According to Morgan, the minutes of the next county commissioners' court meeting stipulated that a new courthouse "shall be built so strong that Jim Dickson's bull or no other damn bull can butt it down."

The next generation of Texas courthouses, those built in the 1850s and '60s, were generally bull-proof frame or brick buildings in the Greek Revival style with white columns out front, modeled on courthouses further east. But as Texas counties grew rich on cotton and cattle in the 1880s and '90s, these courthouses suddenly seemed shabby and old-fashioned, and they were replaced with the Golden Age courthouses. Romanesque and Renaissance Revival wedding cakes with towers and cupolas and mansard roofs and rusticated arches, and all of the exuberant paraphernalia of late Victorian architecture, an architecture that perfectly expressed the period of rampant economic growth that Mark Twain called "The Great Barbecue." These are the courthouses that I love.

The Marfa courthouse is a perfect example of this style. When it was built in 1886, Presidio County was the largest county in the United States, with twelve thousand square miles (but fewer than three thousand people), and the county commissioners wanted a courthouse that would not only reflect that grandeur but would assert Marfa's superiority over Fort Davis, whose run-down adobe courthouse was one of the arguments for moving the Presidio County seat to Marfa the previous year. Although the architect of record was James H. Britton, the courthouse was probably designed by San Antonian Alfred Giles, who designed eight other Texas courthouses built in the 1880s and '90s, as well as banks and public buildings all over Texas and northern Mexico. Giles produced a courthouse that could be seen for miles across the prairie.

Giles was one of several Texas architects who specialized in

courthouses in those years. Another was Wesley Clark Dodson of Waco, whose cluster of Second Empire courthouses in Weatherford, Denton, Granbury, and Hillsboro were the destinations of my earliest courthouse expeditions from Fort Worth in the late 1950s. The most prolific courthouse architect was Dodson's protégée James Riely Gordon, who built eighteen, twelve of which are still standing. The best known are his pink granite and red sandstone confection built in 1895 in Waxahachie and a slightly smaller near-duplicate built the next year in Decatur, which has my great-grandfather's name on the cornerstone because he was a Wise County commissioner that year. Gordon also built the polychrome Fayette County courthouse in La Grange, which incorporates blue sandstone, red sandstone, pink granite, and white limestone and has a palm court with a cast iron fountain in its center.

Gordon was somewhat manipulative in his dealings with county commissioners. When the Fayette County Commissioners Court met in March 1890 to declare the old courthouse unsafe and unanimously voted to build a new one, Gordon was at the meeting and stepped forward to sketch out a rough plan for the new one. The commissioners awarded him the contract without competitive bidding. When it came time to demolish the old courthouse, which had been built thirty-five years earlier by a German stonemason, it took dynamite to get the "unsafe" structure down. The old courthouse cost $14,500; the new one, $100,000. In 1898, the Comal County commissioners retained Gordon to help them draw up the rules for a competition to design a new courthouse in New Braunfels. Gordon suggested that instead of having a competition they go and look at other courthouses and then hire the architect who designed the one they liked best. They got on the train and went down to San Antonio, where they saw Gordon's Bexar County courthouse, and then over to La Grange, where they saw his Fayette County courthouse, and then up to Giddings, where they saw his Lee County courthouse, and then came back to New Braunfels and hired Gordon. He did-n't even have to draw up a new set of plans. He gave them a dupli-cate of the Lee County courthouse, but in limestone instead of brick.

Texas has 254 courthouses, so there is at least one to suit every architectural taste. There are dignified Neo-Classical courthouses and restrained Art Moderne courthouses and even glass boxes from the 1960s. But give me the excessive enthusiasm of the Golden Age courthouses. To me, they exemplify the spirit of Texas.

March 29, 2007

✧ 36 ✧

SNOOPING AROUND
HISTORIC HOUSES

I HAVE ALWAYS BEEN a fan of historic houses, perhaps because I am a born snoop. It is very difficult for me to pass a sign that says "Historic Smedley Jones House, 1840" without stopping to see what kind of stuff the Smedley Joneses had. There are about five thousand historic houses in the United States and sometimes I feel as though I have been in at least half of them.

I discovered early on that there are two kinds of historic houses. I think of them as layered houses and instant houses. Not all layered houses are open to the public. I have a cousin in Austin, a maiden lady in her eighties, who lives in a layered house. It is a big yellow brick house with white columns, built by her grandfather in the 1870s, and everything that was ever brought through the front door is still in it, including two sets of horsehair-covered parlor furniture that were wedding presents given to her grandparents shortly after the Civil War. Also in that parlor is a Gothic table radio from the 1930s, a cabinet hi-fi set from the '50s, and a color TV. Hanging on the wall in the hallway is a framed photograph of her great-grandfather in his Confederate uniform, with the blood-stained sash he was wearing when he was wounded at Gettysburg draped over the frame. Next to the photograph are some ceramic plaques depicting ballet dancers that my cousin made when she was a little girl. Those are layers of history, and there is something very immediate and moving about them.

Not far from my cousin's house is a historic house called the French Legation, which is open to the public. It was built in the

1840s, when Austin was the capital of the Republic of Texas, and it may have been for a few months the residence of an old fraud who called himself Count Jean Pierre Dubois de Saligny, although he was neither a count nor named Saligny. He was, however, the French minister to the Republic of Texas, and for that reason the house was restored in the 1950s by the Daughters of the Republic of Texas and opened to the public as the French Legation Museum. The DRT ladies put together a fine collection of furniture from the 1840s and created an open-hearth kitchen with more brass and copper in it than you would find in a brass foundry, but the whole thing has a glossy look about it that simply does not ring true. It has no continuity. It is a stage set, an instant house.

My favorite layered house is in Washington, DC, and it is open to the public. Tudor Place was built in 1805 by Thomas Peter and his wife, Martha Custis Peter, who was Martha Washington's granddaughter. It was occupied by six generations of the Peter family and, as they say, stuff piled up. Like a lot of layered houses, it had one owner who lived there a long, long time and never changed anything. One of Thomas and Martha Peter's daughters, Britannia Peter Kennon (she had a sister named America), was born in the house in 1815. She was married in 1842, was widowed fourteen months later, and returned to Tudor Place to spend the rest of her life there. During the Civil War she saved the house from confiscation as a hospital by renting rooms to influential Union army officers—even though she was Robert E. Lee's cousin. She died in 1911, a day short of her ninety-sixth birthday.

I was in the house shortly after the last owner, Armistead Peter III, died in 1983. It was stuffed with three centuries worth of furniture. In Armistead Peter's study there was a massive partners' desk from the 1880s, which Peter used daily, but pushed against the west wall was an eighteenth-century secretary desk that might have been at Mount Vernon. On Peter's desk was a telephone from the 1960s, but it was wired into an outlet in the ceiling that was attached to an electric chandelier that was installed about 1890. In the garage was a 1919 Pierce-Arrow roadster with a rumble seat, which Peter drove around Washington until the 1970s. Tudor Place is a historic house with innumerable layers.

But you don't need to go all the way to Washington to see a layered historic house. The Magoffin House in El Paso, which is operated by the Texas Parks and Wildlife Department, is a fine example. It is a very large adobe house, built in 1875 by Joseph Magoffin and lived in by his descendants for the next 110 years. Joseph Magoffin was one of the wealthiest men in El Paso, a real-estate tycoon who inherited a great chunk of El Paso from his father, Santa Fe trader James Magoffin. He could buy anything that could be shipped over the railroad to El Paso and he did. Even though the house was a flat-roofed adobe, Magoffin's wife and daughter decorated it like a Fifth Avenue mansion, with Arts-and-Crafts wallpaper, Brussels carpets, a five-piece parlor set, a 26-place dining table, and an incredible bedroom suite purchased at the New Orleans Cotton Exposition of 1884. Magoffin lived there until his death in 1927. His daughter, Josephine Magoffin Glasgow, then moved into the house with her husband, a retired army general who for a number of years was the oldest living grad-uate of West Point. They added a layer of furniture they had acquired during a lifetime of military service, and the whole ensemble was then preserved by their unmarried daughter Octavia, who lived in the house until her death in 1968. The Glasgows remodeled the house in the Santa Fe style, pulling down the wallpaper and tearing out the canvas ceilings to expose the log beams, but the Parks and Wildlife recently restored the house to its 1900 appearance, and the result is breathtaking.

October 5, 2006

❖ 37 ❖

JUNETEENTH BELONGS TO TEXAS

LAST MONTH I was rambling around the Hill Country, working on a research project that has occupied most of my spring and summer, and stopped for breakfast at the Bowling Alley Café on the square in Blanco, a small town on US 281 between Johnson City and San Antonio. Taped to the door of the café was a handbill advertising the annual Juneteenth celebration at Peyton Colony, an African American community about five miles east of Blanco. I have lived in Far West Texas for so long that I had almost forgotten about Juneteenth, but in the parts of our state that have large African American populations it is a red-letter day, a uniquely Texan holiday.

Juneteenth, or, as it is sometimes more formally designated, June the Nineteenth, commemorates the day in June 1865 when the Federal General Gordon Granger issued a proclamation at his headquarters in Galveston that succinctly stated, "The people of Texas are informed that, in accordance with a proclamation from the Executive of the United States, all slaves are free." The descendants of those slaves still celebrate that day with fervor.

The "proclamation from the Executive" that General Granger was referring to was, of course, Abraham Lincoln's Emancipation Proclamation, issued on January 1, 1863. Since that proclamation only applied to slaves held in the states that were in rebellion against the Union, it was not effective until those states were occupied by Federal troops. In Texas that did not occur until after the end of the war. Various folk tales have arisen to explain the delay.

I have heard it said that although the white planters of Texas knew about Lincoln's proclamation as soon as it was issued, they held the news back from their slaves for two and a half years so that they could get three more cotton crops in. Another story is that Lincoln gave a black Union soldier a mule and started him off through the South to bring the slaves news of their freedom, and his mule was so slow that he did not reach Texas until June 19, 1865.

In fact, issuing the proclamation was Granger's first order of business after Galveston was occupied, and the spontaneous celebrations started as the news spread from one plantation to the next. By the late 1860s, the holiday had been institutionalized by the Freedman's Bureau, whose agents used it to teach the assembled crowds about their new voting rights. After the Bureau's demise in 1870, Juneteenth took on a life of its own. The celebrations frequently took place on grounds that had been purchased by African American associations for that purpose, such as Austin's Emancipation Park and Mexia's thirty-acre Comanche Crossing, purchased by the Mexia Nineteenth of June Association.

The earliest celebrations always included a church service, held outdoors or in a tabernacle, and that has remained an important part of Juneteenth in most places. Another fixed element is a barbecue lunch with all the trimmings, including potato salad, beans, and mustard and collard greens. The food is always abundant, in contrast to the short rations endured by the participants' enslaved ancestors, and is usually free. In 1918 the Austin paper reported that "beer, a hog, and two muttons" had been purchased with donations for the Juneteenth celebration; today the fare is more likely to be iced tea and chicken, sausage, and ribs. In 1933 a participant described a recent Juneteenth meal to folklorist William Wiggins: "The dinner was free. And you got all you wanted to eat. They had rows and rows of long, long tables. The young men usually served as waiters, and the young ladies served as waitresses. No part of the dinner was sold, but they did buy the cold drinks and ice cream." These days the meal is usually followed by a baseball game, a concert, or an evening dance. Sometimes a reading of the Emancipation Proclamation or of General Granger's proclamation is part of the program.

It has always been a tradition to dress up for Juneteenth. In the 1920s and '30s Houston department stores ran ads in the local African American newspaper, the *Informer,* urging readers to buy new clothes at low prices. "DRESS UP AS YOU SHOULD BE FOR JUNETEENTH," was the headline on an ad from Landers, which offered men's suits for "one-fourth down and the balance as you are paid." Today most of older men at a Juneteenth celebration will be dressed in dark suits and ties, and the women will wear good dresses and flowery hats.

Juneteenth also functions as a homecoming and a family reunion. In the 1920s and '30s the railroads ran special excursion trains to the big celebrations, such as the one at Mexia, which lasted three days and attracted as many as thirty thousand people. At the earliest celebrations, the religious ceremonies always included testimonials by former slaves who related their trials under slavery and gave thanks for their freedom. Today, a retelling of family histories and a reaffirmation of family continuity is an important part of Juneteenth, especially since so many young people who have moved from Texas to distant cities return for the celebration.

In the past few years there has been a movement to make Juneteenth a national holiday honoring African American emancipation. There is an organization called the National Juneteenth Holiday Campaign, which has lobbied to have Juneteenth recognized as an official state holiday in twenty-nine states (it became one in Texas in 1980), as well as a federal holiday. Juneteenth celebrations were held this year in such widely scattered spots as Los Angeles, Minneapolis, and Mount Vernon, New York. They featured jazz concerts, beauty contests, car shows, health fairs, and poetry readings, as well as religious services and barbecue dinners.

But Juneteenth's roots remain in Texas. The handbill that I saw in Blanco advertising the Peyton Colony celebration gave the program. It read: "11:00—Worship service, all welcome; 12:00—Tours of church and school; 1:00 to 3:00—Serving barbecue, no fee; 7:00-End? We'll end when we can't play no more." That's a real Juneteenth, and I was sorry that I couldn't be there for it.

July 10, 2008

38

CHRISTMAS IN ANSON

THERE ARE TWO poems that every Texan of my parents' generation knew by heart and would recite at the drop of a hat. They are Frank Deprez's "Lasca" and Larry Chittenden's "The Cowboys' Christmas Ball." Not long ago I ran into Chuck Finsley, retired curator of paleontology at the Dallas Museum of Science, who was having lunch with my friend Evelyn Luciani at the Food Shark in Marfa. Finsley was in town to plan a bus tour of the Big Bend for a group of Dallasites and he was trying to persuade Luciani to join the tour and recite "Lasca" as the bus rolled down US 67 from Marfa to Presidio. The poem, in the best sentimental Victorian tradition, is about a Texas rancher who is saved from a stampede by his lover who throws her body over his and is trampled to death by the cattle. The last line goes, "Does half my heart lie buried there, down by the Rio Grande?"

But because Christmas is coming this column is about the other poem, "The Cowboys' Christmas Ball," which has detached itself from the printed page and taken on a life of its own. The poem, which describes a dance held in Anson City, Texas, in the late 1880s, was written by Larry Chittenden, a local rancher, and was first published in the Anson City newspaper, the *Texas Western*, in June 1890. The Star Hotel, where the dance was held, had just burned down, and the newspaper was seeking information about the hotel's history. "The Cowboys' Christmas Ball" was Chittenden's contribution. Three years later it was included in a volume of Chittenden's poetry called *Ranch Verses*, published by G. P. Putnam's Sons in New York. *Ranch Verses* went through sixteen printings and earned Chittenden the sobriquet "The Poet Ranchman." It also brought "The Cowboys' Christmas Ball" to a national audience.

The poem, in six verses of jogging, slangy lines that are reminiscent of Robert Service's poems of the Far North, lends itself both to recitation and to singing. Someone probably set it to music soon after it was published, because it appeared in the first book of cowboy songs, Jack Tharp's *Songs of the Cowboys* (1908). Tharp's book also included a knockoff of Chittenden's poem called "The Cowboys' New Year's Dance," set in Roswell, New Mexico, and supposedly written by Mark Chisholm, a clever pseudonym that calls up both Mark Twain and the Chisholm Trail. John A. Lomax included Chittenden's verses in the 1916 edition of his *Cowboy Songs*, saying that it "had been set to music by cowboys." In 1946 a cowboy singer named Gordon Graham wrote a new tune for it, and in 1985 Michael Martin Murphey made a hit recording of the song to that tune. The poem has also been reprinted hundreds of times in magazines, usually at Christmas, and it became a standard recitation piece at Christmas celebrations.

The Christmas dance that Chittenden described was held sporadically in Anson until Prohibition. In 1934, however, a local English teacher, Leonora Barrett, aware of the poem's popularity, decided to revive the dance as a historical pageant. Barrett was a student of J. Frank Dobie's, and she had written her University of Texas master's thesis on "The Texas Cowboy in Literature." She organized a group of dancers who could perform waltzes, schottisches, reels, and polkas, dressed them in Victorian costumes, took over the high school gymnasium, and the Cowboys' Christmas Ball was reborn. Three years later Barrett took the dancers to the National Folk Festival in Chicago; they were such a hit that when the festival was held in Washington, DC, in 1938, they were invited to dance on the White House lawn. In 1940 the Works Progress Administration built a rock building in Anson, Pioneer Hall, as a permanent home for the ball, which still takes place there on three nights every December. Shortly after Michael Martin Murphey recorded the song, he more or less adopted the ball, and his annual appearance there has swelled the number of dancers considerably.

Larry Chittenden, the poem's author and spiritual father of the ball, was hardly your typical Texas rancher. His father was a prominent New York dry goods merchant, and Chittenden started his career as a clerk in his father's store. He first came to Texas to manage a ranch in Jones County that his uncle, a congressman from New York, had bought. He stayed in Texas about fifteen years and then moved to Bermuda. There he produced another volume of poetry, *Bermuda Verses*, which contains lines like *Bright land of lovely lilies, roses, and cedar trees / Enchantment dwells about thee and in thy emerald seas.* "The Cowboys' Christmas Ball" may be his best poem. He ended up in Christmas Cove, Maine, where he established a public library of autographed books. He died in 1934.

This year's Cowboys' Christmas Ball will be held in Anson on December 16, 17, and 18. Suanne Holtman, who has been involved with the ball for eighteen years ("and I'm a newcomer," she says), tells me that there are still plenty of tickets at $15 each. However, there are certain rules that dancers must observe in order to preserve the decorum of the 1880s. Ladies must wear skirts on the dance floor (and no split skirts) and men must not dance with their hats on (there will be a hat check booth). No alcohol is permitted, although Holtman says, "What people drink in their cars between dances is their own business." The ball will be opened by a grand march at 9:00 p.m. each evening, and the dances will include waltzes, schottisches, Virginia reels, polkas, and a Paul Jones. Michael Martin Murphey will perform on Thursday night, and there will be a box social auction that night, so you can eat supper with your sweetheart.

So get yourself to Anson City, *old Jones's county seat / Where they raised polled Angus cattle and waving whiskered wheat and spend an evening at that lively gaited sworray—the Cowboys' Christmas Ball."*

December 16, 2010

39

THERE WAS NOTHING
FOR US TO DO BUT RUN

THE GREEN, rolling, oak-studded country between the Colorado and Brazos Rivers below Austin and Waco is one of the most beautiful parts of Texas, but in the wet spring of 1836 it was the setting for some of the darkest days in Texas history. During the weeks between March 6 of that year, when the Alamo fell, and April 21, when Santa Anna was defeated at San Jacinto, the Mexican army moved eastward from San Antonio into the heart of Anglo-American Texas, destroying everything in its path, and Sam Houston's army retreated before it. No one knew what the outcome would be.

"There was nothing for us to do but run," recalled Lucinda Gorham, recounting the events of forty years earlier. "We went to Cunninghams to join the Bastrop people, who were going by the Gotcher Trace. We camped in the field, and before daylight twenty-five Comanches stampeded and took our horses. We put it to a vote whether we should stop there and send to the army for relief, or get away from there as fast as we could. The women voted, too."

Lucinda Gorham was recalling the Runaway Scrape, the mass flight of Anglo-American settlers to the Sabine River, the boundary between Mexican Texas and American Louisiana, which took place during those weeks. She told her story to Julia Lee Sinks in 1876, when Sinks was interviewing old settlers for a history of Fayette County. Her brief narrative captures the fear, indecision, and misery that accompanied the panic that swept through the Anglo settlements of Texas that spring. Gorham went on to tell

Sinks that after the Comanches ran their horses off, her little group made a stand on the prairie, the men waving their rifles and the women waving sticks, hoping that the Comanches would mistake them for rifles. The Comanches emerged from the woods on horseback and circled the group several times but did not attack them, eventually riding off to loot a nearby cotton gin. Lucinda Gorham and her group got across the Colorado River in an abandoned boat and walked across Fayette and Washington counties to the Brazos in knee-deep mud. When they got to the crossing at Washington-on-the-Brazos, they found the west bank of the river jammed "with all manner of vehicles, good and worn-out carriages, ox and mule wagons, trucks, slides, anything that could carry women and children."

The panic started at Gonzales on March 11, the day the news of the fall of the Alamo reached Sam Houston and the Texas army that was camped there. The slaughter at the Alamo created twenty widows in that little town, many of them young women with small children. Houston ordered the army to withdraw eastward and the town to be burned, and the women and children followed the army.

As Houston's little army retreated toward the Colorado River, the panic spread across Texas as the word flew from settlement to settlement that Santa Anna's army meant to purge the region of Anglo-Americans. In Nacogdoches, far from the Mexican threat, the rumor started that the Cherokees had allied themselves with the Mexicans and were planning to massacre the population. Most of the men were on their way to join the army, and colonist John A. Quitman reported that "the houses are all deserted and there are several thousands of women and children in the woods on both sides of the Sabine without supplies or money."

In fact the Runaway Scrape was almost entirely an exodus of women and children. As Houston's army crossed first the Colorado and then the Brazos without making a stand, retreating further and further eastward, more and more farms were abandoned and ever-increasing numbers of women whose men were with the army took to the roads with their children. The rains that spring were the heaviest in many years. The roads turned into quagmires and the rivers and creeks swelled beyond their banks. Dilue Rose Harris, who was eleven years old when her family abandoned their home at Stafford's Point, recalled that when they reached the San Jacinto River at Lynch's Ferry there were five thousand people waiting to cross. They camped in the rain for three days before they could get to the other side. They pushed on east to the Trinity River, which was out of its banks and covered with driftwood. "The horrors of crossing the Trinity are beyond my power to describe," she later wrote. "Measles, sore eyes, whooping cough, and every other disease that man, woman, or child is heir to broke out among us." It took them five days to cross the swollen river and get out of its flooded bottom. Her little sister died in her mother's arms and was buried in the cemetery at Liberty, where a family took them in. They were so exhausted they could go no further.

They were still at Liberty when they heard a sound like distant thunder. It was the cannons firing at San Jacinto. The cannonading was so brief that they thought that the Texans had been defeated, and they started east again, only to be overtaken by a man on horseback who shouted, "Turn back! No danger! The Texans have whipped the Mexican army!" She recalled that her mother laughed that night for the first time since they left home. Mary Helm, another refugee, remembered that when news of the victory reached their camp, her party "all turned shouting Methodist . . . some danced, some laughed, some clapped their hands."

For many, the trip back home was as arduous as the flight. The rain was unrelenting, the rivers were still up, and the roads were still morasses. When they reached their homes they found them in ashes. Santa Anna's army had burned everything in its path. Rosa von Roeder Kleberg recalled that when her family left their home at Cat Spring they had buried their large library, but the Mexicans found it and tore the pages from all the books as well as burning their home. "We had to begin anew," she wrote, "with less than we had when we started."

For those who were in it, the Runaway Scrape became a watershed that divided old Texans from Johnny-come-latelies. This year, as Texans mark the 175th anniversary of the Texas Revolution, the Runaway Scrape seems to have fallen between the cracks, forgotten amidst celebrations of the Declaration of Independence, the Alamo, and San Jacinto. But it should be remembered and celebrated, too, because it is a monument to the fortitude of Texas women, who held their families together in the face of disaster.

April 14, 2011

✤ 40 ✤

SAN ANTONIO'S CEMENT SCULPTURE

VISITORS TO San Antonio sometimes comment on a peculiar bus stop shelter on Broadway just north of its intersection with Hildebrand, in front of one of the gates to the campus of Immaculate Word University. At first glance it looks like something out of a Mexican jungle, a thatched roof supported by three thick tree trunks rising from a floor of half-sawn logs, with backless split-log benches around the base of each tree trunk. Except that the whole thing is made out of textured and colored concrete.

Not far away in Brackenridge Park is a footbridge that resembles a long arbor. Thirty-three pairs of tree trunks face each other on either side of a plank floor, their branches interlocking above, each trunk joined to the next by log handrails. The logs are riddled with knotholes and insect borings and have patches where the bark has been stripped from them. The tree trunks, the branches, the handrails, and the plank floor are all concrete.

Just up Hildebrand from the bus shelter is a small city park called Miraflores Park, all that is left of a fifteen-acre private garden built in the 1920s by Dr. Aureliano Urrutia, a San Antonio physician whose mansion was nearby. One of the gates to the park is an archway cut into a hollow tree, which leads to twelve crosscut log steps that curve downward into the park. Once more, all concrete.

These monumental curiosities are all the work of Dionicio Rodriguez, a native of Mexico who was a master of the concrete-working technique known in Spanish as *trabajo rustico* (rustic work) and in French as *faux bois* (imitation wood). Rodriguez came to San Antonio from Mexico in 1924 to work on Dr. Urrutia's garden, went on to ornament other parts of San Antonio and to jobs in several other cities in Texas, and traveled with his crew to execute projects across the country until his death in 1955. His somewhat bizarre work is in the aesthetic tradition of miniature golf courses, but it is technically perfect, and it has always attracted the attention of fans whose initial reaction is usually, "Who in the world would do something like that?"

Now that question has been answered in a new book by Patsy Pittman Light, *Capturing Nature: the Cement Sculpture of Dionicio Rodriguez*, published by Texas A&M Press. Light, who is an ardent historic preservationist, became fascinated by Rodriguez's bus stop shelter and Brackenridge Park bridge when she moved to San Antonio forty-five years ago. In 1995 some of Rodriguez's work at San Antonio's Alamo Cement Company headquarters, including a 125-foot-long fence incorporating twenty varieties of tree bark and a fountain ornamented with concrete cactus plants, was threatened with destruction when the property they were on was sold to a developer to become a shopping center. The San Antonio Conservation Society stepped in to save them, and Light wrote National Register of Historic Places nominations for them. The research that she did for those nominations started her on a ten-year quest for information about the mysterious Rodriguez, and *Capturing Nature* is the result.

Light's research led her not only to examples of Rodriguez's work all over the country but to some very peculiar clients. In Port Arthur, Texas, she learned about a tugboat captain, Ambrose Eddingston, who hired Rodriguez to build ornamental structures in an apartment complex he was developing. Eddingston gave Rodriguez five thousand conch shells that he had imported from his native Cayman Islands, and Rodriguez used them to build a shell-encrusted wall and gate and a grotto called the Cave of a

Thousand Sounds whose interior is covered with conch shells. In North Little Rock, Arkansas, she encountered real estate developer Justin Matthews, who hired Rodriguez to ornament a park in one of his developments with a full-sized nineteenth-century stone mill, whose concrete machinery is powered by a ten-thousand-pound concrete waterwheel. In Memphis she found out about Clovis Hinds, a cemetery developer who, inspired by Los Angeles's Forest Lawn Cemetery, retained Rodriguez to create cement representations of Biblical sites, including Abraham's Oak, the Cave of Machpelah, and the Pool of Hebron, as well as the non-Biblical Annie Laurie Wishing Chair, at his Memorial Park Cemetery.

Rodriguez did not draw up plans or keep written records of his work, so Light was dependent on oral sources for information about his techniques and methods. She was able to find several men who had worked with him, including his great-nephew Carlos Cortes, who continued the tradition of Rodriguez's work in San Antonio. But her most valuable source was Rodriguez's niece, Manuela Vargas Theall, who had traveled with Rodriguez and his crew in the 1930s and had kept a box of photographs and correspondence. The man who emerges from these interviews is a dapper, somewhat vain, exacting, and secretive craftsman, who was prosperous enough to buy a new car every year during the Depression. According to his niece, Rodriguez always wore a three-piece suit and a dress shirt with cufflinks and a tie. When he went to work, he took off his coat and pulled on coveralls and galoshes. His crew built the armatures for his structures and applied the first layers of cement under his direction, but it was Rodriguez who applied the final layer and added the color and the texture. He mixed his colors in the trunk of his car or in a little tent, and would not let anyone come near him while he was doing it, fearful that one of his crew might learn his techniques and go into competition with him. When he got old, he paid neighborhood boys a penny each to pluck out the white hairs from his head.

Rodriguez's skill with cement and color enabled him to create unique monuments that rank with Sam Rodia's Watts Towers, Leonard Knight's Salvation Mountain, and other visionary environments. When Patsy Light first contacted Manuela Vargas Theall, Theall said, "I always hoped that my uncle would be famous." Now, thanks to Light's research and the beautiful color photographs which illustrate her book, he will be.

April 13, 2008

✤ 41 ✤

THE FLYING BOAT
ON MEDINA LAKE

THE NEW YEAR always makes me think of Aggie Pate and his calendars. A. M. "Aggie" Pate Jr. was a Fort Worth businessman who had an interest in the history of transportation and in the 1960s founded the Pate Museum of Transportation, a collection of automobiles, helicopters, airplanes, and even a homemade submarine. Pate had a healthy ego. For a number of years his company, Panther Oil and Grease, put out an annual calendar entitled "Great Moments in Transportation History." The calendar featured illustrations of events such as the arrival of Lindbergh at Le Bourget airport in Paris and the Wright brothers' first flight at Kitty Hawk. The illustrations were based on photographs, but Pate had the artist paint him, Aggie Pate, into each scene, so that as Lindbergh was climbing out of his cockpit at Le Bourget there was Pate, hand outstretched, among the officials waiting to greet him.

One event in transportation history that Pate's calendars missed was the attempt of the Italian aviator Colonel Francesco de Pinedo to free his flying boat from the waters of Lake Medina, near San Antonio, Texas, on April 3, 1927. While this might not have been exactly a Great Moment, it was a turning point in aviation history, and it happened right here in Texas.

At the time, Colonel de Pinedo was one of the most famous aviators in the world. In the 1920s the Italians pioneered the development of flying boats—airplanes that could land on water but not on land—and in 1925 Colonel de Pinedo flew one on a thirty-four-thousand-mile trip from Italy to Japan to Australia and back.

He became an Italian national hero, and men all over Italy sported Pinedo jackets—double-breasted, sky blue wool blazers. In 1927, he persuaded Mussolini to send him on a tour of South and North America that would demonstrate the superiority of the Italian aircraft industry and the Italian Air Force, and that would make him the first foreign military pilot to fly across the Atlantic to the United States.

For his flight de Pinedo chose a Savoia S.55 flying boat, a weird-looking machine that consisted of two huge hollow pontoons connected by a seventy-eight-foot wing, with a stabilizer and three upright rudders extended behind the pontoons on a pair of booms. Two engines were mounted back-to-back on struts above the wing, with one propeller facing forward and one backward. The cockpit, which held the pilot and two crew members, was inside the leading edge of the wing, and twelve passengers could ride inside the pontoons, which had portholes in their sides. De Pinedo named his plane the *Santa Maria*, after Columbus's flagship.

De Pinedo and his crew took off from Cagliari, Sardinia, on February 13, 1927, and flew to Rabat, Morocco, and then down the coast of West Africa to Dakar and across the Atlantic to Natal, Brazil. From there they flew south along the Brazilian coast to Montevideo, Uruguay, and then turned north across the interior of Brazil, landing on lakes and rivers, to Georgetown in British Guiana; and from there across the Caribbean and the Gulf of Mexico to New Orleans. They arrived in New Orleans just after noon on March 29, having flown the seven hundred miles from Havana in six and a half hours. According to the *New York Times*, de Pinedo climbed out of the cockpit clean shaven and wearing golf knickers. He told reporters that he had shaved at fifteen hundred feet and that he carried a phonograph in the cockpit with him and listened to American foxtrots while flying. He was clearly a showman.

De Pinedo and his crew were given a tremendous reception in New Orleans, which included a mass of thanksgiving at St. Louis Cathedral and a banquet hosted by the Italian consulate. Three days later he took off for San Antonio, then the seat of United States military aviation. The only place near San Antonio that the *Santa Maria* could land was Medina Lake, a long, narrow, man-made lake about twenty miles from town, and that was where de Pinedo set the plane down. A large crowd lined the shoreline, including a delegation of Italian American children from San Antonio wearing the black shirts of Mussolini's Fascist Party. General Frank Lahm, the chief of military aviation in San Antonio, went out to the *Santa Maria* in a launch to greet de Pinedo; the plane was towed to a dock and moored, and everyone went into town to party.

The next morning was not a good day for Italian aviation. Under the eyes of the top brass of the US Army Air Corps, the *Santa Maria* refused to lift off from the placid waters of Lake Medina. There was no wind, and the surface tension of the calm lake was too great for the flying boat's pontoons to break away from. After several futile runs up and down the lake, de Pinedo gave up and decided to try again the next day. The next morning the same thing happened, but someone had the bright idea of running several speedboats in front of the plane and creating enough wave action to provide the needed lift. De Pinedo soared away to his next destination, Elephant Butte Lake in New Mexico. He flew due west from San Antonio to Del Rio and then followed the Rio Grande to Elephant Butte, so he must have passed over the Big Bend. He arrived safely at Elephant Butte, but when he tried to take off from that lake the next morning he once again found his plane surface bound, and the motorboats had to be brought out again.

De Pinedo's next stop was Roosevelt Lake near Phoenix, Arizona, and there real disaster struck. While the *Santa Maria* was being refueled before a crowd of spectators it burst into flames, and de Pinedo and his crew watched it burn to the waterline. Italian newspapers screamed that it was anti-Fascist sabotage, and an international incident loomed, but it turned out that a boy in a boat next to the plane had lit a cigarette and carelessly tossed the match into the gasoline-filmed water.

Mussolini sent de Pinedo a replacement airplane, christened the *Santa Maria II*, and de Pinedo started home in that, but the prestige of Italian aviation had been dealt a crippling blow by the lakes of the Southwest. To add insult to injury, while de Pinedo was crossing Newfoundland in the *Santa Maria II*, headed for the Atlantic, Charles Lindbergh landed in Paris, and the Italians and their flying boats disappeared entirely from the newspapers. The aviation world quickly concluded that flying boats were not suited for traversing the arid portions of the earth.

January 8, 2009

✢ 42 ✢

DANCE HALLS AND HONKY TONKS

I SPENT A RECENT weekend at a symposium on the preservation of Texas dance halls, held at the James Dick Festival Institute in Round Top, Texas, and cosponsored by Texas Dance Hall Preservation, Inc. I learned a lot. I learned, for instance, that it is hard to distinguish what is a dance hall and what is not. If you made a graph of dance halls as a series of concentric circles, there would be an inner circle of halls that were built by German, Czech, Polish, and Mexican immigrant groups, where regularly scheduled dances sponsored by the organization that built the hall take place. These would be surrounded by a layer of commercial dance halls like the Cotton Club in Lubbock, the Eldorado Ballroom in Houston, and La Villita in Alice, which are essentially nightclubs with dance floors and house bands. Then on the outer edge there would be roadhouses and bars where dancing to live music happens, which the Dance Hall Preservation folks consider honky tonks and somewhat beyond the pale. As Steve Dean, one of the organizers of the preservation group, says, "A dance hall is where you go to dance with your wife. A honky tonk is where you go to dance with someone else's wife."

I learned that the classic Texas dance hall is a big white frame structure out in the country built by a German choral singing society (*Gesaengverein*), gymnastic society (*Turnverein*), or target-shooting club (*Schuetzenverein*), a Mexican *Sociedad Protectiva*, or a Czech fraternal insurance group, the SPJST or its Catholic counterpart, the KJT. According to Patrick Sparks, president of Texas Dance Hall Preservation, Inc., there are about two hundred of these still standing, although many of them are abandoned. In its purest form, the classic hall has three distinctive architectural features: the windows have no glass in them but are covered by hinged shutters which can be raised when the hall is in use, creating an open-air pavilion from which the music wafts out across the surrounding fields; the ceiling is either very high or completely absent, leaving the wooden trusses that support the roof exposed to view; and the beer is dispensed from a separate building on the grounds, freeing up space in the hall for dancing. The La Bahia Turnverein hall at Burton, built in 1902, which our group toured on Sunday morning, is a perfect example: hinged window shutters, exposed rafters, separate beer dispensary. Many other halls from the same period have had their ceilings lowered and glass windows installed so that they can be air-conditioned, to the despair of the preservationists. Dancers at La Bahia are cooled by fans in the shape of airplanes with huge propellers mounted on the rafters, and when the windows are open and the hot air rises to the roof it is quite pleasant.

I learned that the music played in Texas dance halls is a blend of Texas swing, contemporary country western, Mexican *conjunto*, and German, Polish, and Czech polkas. Brian Marshall, who was born in the Polish community of Bremond, Texas, and has a band called the Tex-Slavic Playboys, gave us a demonstration on his fiddle of how this works. He played the Mexican polka "Jesusita en Chihuahua" and its derivative, "The Jesse Polka," and a Polish folk tune that sounded exactly like Eddie Arnold's "Cattle Call." He told us that when he was in his late teens, Houston bandleader Larry Butler called him and invited him to join Butler's band. "I'm not really all that good," Marshall told him. "Can you play 'Faded Love'?" Butler asked. "Yes," Marshall said. "Can you play 'Cotton-Eyed Joe'?" was the next question. "Yes," Marshall said. "Can you play 'Jolie Blonde'?" "Yes." "You're hired," Butler said. "Play each one of those three times each night and you're a country western fiddler." Marshall ended his presentation by playing "Jolie Blonde" on the fiddle and singing the words in Polish, a perfect Texas dance hall blend.

I learned that the barbecued sausage that is a staple of weekend dance hall feasts is not part of the traditional Texas barbecuer's repertoire, but is a product of the twentieth-century Texas cotton industry. Robb Walsh, a Houston food writer who spoke at the symposium, told the audience that traditional Texas barbecue consisted of large chunks, like halves and quarters, of beef, pork, and mutton cooked over coals in long trenches. In the 1880s and '90s, German immigrant butchers began opening meat markets in towns like Giddings, Taylor, Lockhart, and Cuero, and they built raised, covered, German-style meat smokers in their markets so that they could offer their customers smoked meat to take home. As the cotton industry expanded across Texas in the early twentieth century, an army of cotton pickers, largely African Americans or Mexicans, moved north across the state every year, following the cotton crop. On Saturdays the cotton pickers poured into nearby towns. They were excluded from segregated restaurants, but were welcome to buy cooked meat at the meat markets. Sausage was the cheapest available meat, at a dime a link, and a man could make a pretty good meal out of a couple of links of sausage and the free soda crackers that the markets threw in. And so a new Texas barbecue tradition was born, and it quickly moved into the dance halls.

The most important thing that I learned, however, is that the rural Texas dance hall is an endangered species, threatened on the one hand by abandonment and on the other by modernization. There were once over one thousand of them; now only about five hundred of all categories are left. A group of young people—architects, musicians, and people who love dancing—have banded together to save them. They have developed a strategy that is based on generating enthusiasm for the halls and developing preservation guidelines that can be used by local preservation groups. They hope to eventually place a core group of Texas halls on the National Register of Historic Places. You can check out their website at texasdancehall.org. Use it to locate a dance hall, then use their calendar to find out when the next dance there will be, and then go dancing. You'll be doing your part to preserve a hall just by being there.

September 30, 2010

❖ 43 ❖

FIDEL IN WHARTON

IDEL CASTRO has made two trips to Texas. On the first, he went away with money; on the second, with a horse. The second visit was the longest and most public, and it won Fidel the temporary good will of a covey of wealthy Houston businessmen. It was part of a two-week trip that the Cuban premier made to the United States in April 1959, just three months after his revolutionary army entered Havana and overthrew the dictatorship of Fulgencio Batista. Castro was still a romantic hero to most Americans then, a freedom fighter who had just come down from the mountains to cleanse Cuba of corruption. His trip was intended to build up good will and reassure Americans that his revolution was no threat to our national interest. He arrived in Washington, DC, on April 15 with fifty fatigue-clad and bearded comrades, nineteen armed bodyguards, and a hundred cases of rum to be used as gifts.

His visit was not an official one, as he was not yet a head of state. President Eisenhower went on a five-day golfing trip while Castro was in Washington, but Vice President Nixon met with him for two hours. Castro toured the monuments and Mount Vernon, received visitors at the Cuban Embassy, held a press conference, and had dinner at a Chinese restaurant, where he debated with students at nearby tables. From Washington he went to New York, Boston, and Montreal, stopping to address students at Princeton, Harvard, and the Lawrenceville School, creating a sensation with his beard, cigar, fatigues, and gun-toting bodyguards.

Castro's last stop on that trip was Houston. Lyndon Johnson, then a US Senator, asked the Houston Jaycees to invite Castro so that Houston businessmen with interests in Cuba could meet with him. They welcomed him enthusiastically. His party traveled by motorcade with a police escort, sirens screaming, from Hobby Airport to the Shamrock Hilton Hotel. They were met in the lobby by a cheering crowd of Houston businessmen, accompanied by their wives and children. Some of the children were dressed as miniature Cuban rebels, in fatigues and waving little Cuban flags.

That night the Jaycees gave a banquet for the Cubans, attended by Mayor Lewis Cutrer and the cream of River Oaks society. There is a *Houston Chronicle* photograph of Castro enjoying himself at the dinner, wearing his fatigues and a Stetson hat presented to him by oilman Frank B. Waters, gesturing with a cigar in his right hand. One of the other guests that night was wildcatter John B. Ferguson, owner of the world's fastest quarterhorse, Go Man Go, which was stabled at Ferguson's ranch at Mackay. According to Ferguson's daughter, Joan Attaway, Castro and Ferguson got to talking horses, and Ferguson expansively said, "If you're ever back this way come out to my ranch. I want you to have a colt." Castro said, "I'll be there tomorrow."

The next morning twenty-five cars full of Cubans, reporters, and police headed out of Houston to Mackay. Ferguson had agreed to meet Castro for lunch at Peterson's Restaurant in Wharton and then take him to the ranch. Many of the students at Wharton High School, including my cousin Don Middlebrook, cut classes to go to Peterson's that day. Peterson's was not a large or elegant place; its specialty was fried shrimp in a basket. Don still remembers the scene vividly. "It was very crowded," he told me. "There were reporters and a TV crew there. Castro had half a dozen guards with him, their carbines hanging off their shoulders, ready to shoot."

At the ranch, Ferguson's daughter Joan presented the colt to Castro. "He was very polite, very nice," she recalled. "My husband, Buddy, and I walked back to his limo with him and he invited us to come visit him in Cuba." As for the event itself, she said, "It was a tornado. We had a lot of horses and those Cubans were on them, riding them all over the place. The police were shoulder to shoulder. There were press people there from all over the world. I was glad to get rid of them."

When Castro got back to Houston, his brother Raúl was waiting for him at the Shamrock. He had flown from Havana that afternoon, the only time he ever came to the United States. According to reporters, the brothers got into a shouting argument in Castro's suite that night—their voices could be heard down the hall. Historians think that Fidel had summoned Raúl to Houston to tell him to curtail his plans to export the revolution to the rest of South America; a group of Cuban rebels had just attempted an unsuccessful landing in Panama. The next morning Raúl went back to Havana, and Fidel continued on the South American leg of his tour, flying from Houston to Brazil and Argentina. When he finally got back to Havana on May 7, the first thing that he did was to sign an agrarian reform law that expropriated four hundred and eighty thousand acres of American-owned land, some of which belonged to the King Ranch. Castro promptly lost every friend he had made in Houston. But he kept the horse.

Castro's first visit to Texas? That was in September 1956, when he was still in exile in Mexico, and it only lasted a few hours, but it had momentous consequences. Castro was in Mexico City, desperate for funds to carry on his fight against Batista. Carlos Prío Socarrás, a multimillionaire ex-president of Cuba who was living in Miami, indicated that he might help him; Prío Socarrás had been overthrown as president by Batista in 1952. The two agreed to meet at the Hotel Casa de Palmas in McAllen, Texas. Castro reached McAllen by being driven to Reynosa, Tamaulipas, and wading across the Rio Grande. After a few hours conversation, Prío Socarrás gave Castro $100,000 to buy guns and ammunition. Castro slipped back across the river and returned to Mexico City.

Two months later he and his men landed on the coast of Cuba, and his revolution was launched. You might say that it started in Texas.

August 11, 2011

✤ 44 ✤

ADVENTURES IN ALBANY

EVERAL WEEKS AGO I went to Albany to speak to the annual Chamber of Commerce dinner there. I do not mean Albany, the capital of the state of New York, but Albany, the county seat of Shackleford County, Texas, a town of two thousand people about thirty miles northeast of Abilene. I went there at the invitation of Shirley and Clifton Caldwell, who are among the main movers behind the cause of historic preservation in Albany, and who own the Mitre Peak Ranch between Fort Davis and Alpine and so can be counted as local folk here as well as in Albany.

Albany is a strange and wonderful place. When I was a teenager and would drive through there with my father on trips from Fort Worth to West Texas, Dad would always point to the old men whittling on the courthouse steps and say, "See those old gentlemen? They all went to college with F. Scott Fitzgerald." In fact, a number of old ranching families in Albany sent their male offspring to Eastern prep schools and then to Princeton, providing the little town with a group of well-educated community leaders for several generations.

One of the best-known Albanians was Watt Matthews, Princeton class of 1921, who died in 1997 at the age of ninety-eight. Matthews was the youngest of the nine children of John and Sallie Reynolds Matthews, whose respective families settled in the Albany area in the 1860s and intermarried to the point that Sallie Reynolds Matthews's history of the region is called *Interwoven*. Watt Matthews came home from Princeton to his family's fifty-thousand-acre Lambshead Ranch and never left it, managing it from his father's death in 1941 until the day of his own death fifty-six years later. He held a number of his Princeton class reunions at the ranch, which is about twenty miles from Albany. Shirley Caldwell told me that you never knew who you would meet at Lambshead; on one occasion Matthews called her and Clifton and said, "Come out here to the ranch for supper; there are some folks here I want you to meet." They went and found themselves having supper with the US Ambassador to the Soviet Union, who was a friend of Matthews's nephew, John Burns. On another occasion they answered a last minute invitation and discovered Lyndon and Lady Bird Johnson sitting in the Lambshead living room. Matthews, who never married, had a remarkable capacity for friendship as well as for ranch management; when he was buried at Lambshead, seven hundred people attended his funeral.

Another Princetonian who had a great influence on Albany was Robert Nail, class of 1933. Robert Nail's family owned a ranch outside of Albany that sat over what, when it was discovered in the 1920s, was the largest shallow-well oil field in the world, and it provided the Nails with enough income to develop their talents. At Princeton Robert Nail discovered that he had a talent for the theater, and after graduation he tried his hand in New York for a while, and directed community theaters in Dallas and Fort Worth. But in 1938 he came home to Albany and wrote the *Fort Griffin Fandangle*, a musical historical pageant that, seventy years later, is still being performed annually in Albany. The *Fandangle* was inspired by productions like Paul Green's "symphonic drama" *The Lost Colony*, but the music, much of it composed by Nail and Watt Matthews's cousin Alice Reynolds, has the lilting quality of a Rodgers and Hammerstein production, and the whole show has a homegrown quality that sets it apart from the slicker summertime theatricals that flourish in places like Branson, Missouri. The script is loosely based on Sallie Reynolds Matthews's book *Interwoven*. Anyone who grew up in Shackleford County can be in it, and the cast and crew has grown over the years to about four hundred people. One of the features of the production is a steam calliope built by an Albany man, who also built the stagecoach and the portable blacksmith shop used in the pageant. The *Fandangle* changes a little each year as new songs and scenes are added and old ones dropped. It runs for two weekends in June and is attended by about ten thousand people every summer.

Robert Nail's nephew Reilly Nail, also a Princeton graduate, collected art, and in 1980 he and his cousin Bill Bomar combined their art collections with those of their mothers to establish the Old Jail Art Center in Albany, making Albany the only town in Texas with a population of two thousand people to have a Modigliani, a Renoir, several Picassos, a Klee, a sculpture by Henry Moore, and a first-class selection of ancient Chinese and pre-Columbian art in its public museum. Not only that, the collections are housed in a limestone building erected in 1877 to serve as Shackleford County's first jail. Across the street from it is the Shackleford County courthouse, a magnificent Second Empire building topped by an impressive clock tower. This was the first Texas courthouse to be restored under the Texas Historical Commission's Texas Historic Courthouse Preservation Program, which is not surprising since the program was the brainchild of Shirley Caldwell, who was a member of the Commission for twelve years and who has encouraged the restoration of buildings all over town.

The Chamber of Commerce dinner at which I spoke was attended by nearly two hundred people. I sat in awe as awards were given out for Historic Preservationist of the Year, Woman of the Year, Citizen of the Year, Rancher of the Year, Teacher of the Year, and so on down the line, marveling that 10 percent of the town's population would attend such an event and that so many people would be deserving of so many awards. When I commented on this to Shirley Caldwell, she said, "You know, I think it's the *Fandangle*. Over the years working on the *Fandangle* has taught us the value of volunteerism, from childhood up. And it's also taught us that we have to cooperate with each other to get anything done."

After the last award was given out, the dinner closed with everyone standing and singing a song called "Prairie Land," whose chorus goes *A prairie plain, a bright blue sky / A snow-white cloud goes sailing high / A wanton wind is blowing free / This is the land for men like me.* It was written by Robert Nail in 1938, and everyone knew the words because it is the closing number of the *Fandangle* and is sung by the entire cast.

April 16, 2009

✤ 45 ✤

THE WEST TEXAS TOWN
OF EL PASO

IN THE SUMMER of 1879, a
forty-six-year-old ex-Confederate
colonel named George Wythe Baylor started out from San
Antonio on horseback to take a new job in El Paso. The job, which
paid $75 a month, was a lieutenancy in the Texas Rangers. Baylor
later wrote that as he had a family and "had been about two years
on scant rations and no pay," he was glad to get it.

Baylor made the 638-mile trip in style. While he rode horseback, his wife, his two daughters (one fourteen and one four), and
his sister-in-law traveled in a hack drawn by two mules, followed by
a wagon packed with a piano, a cookstove, household furnishings,
trunks, and a coop of fighting chickens. Behind that wagon was a
second wagon loaded with groceries for the trip and forage for the
animals. A two-wheeled cart, carrying two men who were bound
for New Mexico and did not want to travel alone, brought up the
rear. Five mounted rangers escorted the group. Tom Lea's lumi-
nous painting "Ranger Escort West of the Pecos" depicts Baylor's
caravan traversing the desert west of the Quitman Mountains. It
was used by the University of Texas Press on the jacket of the 1965
edition of Walter Prescott Webb's *The Texas Rangers.*

Baylor's party spent six weeks on the journey, following the old
military road from San Antonio to El Paso. At Howard's Wells, near
present-day Ozona, they saw the remains of a government wagon
train that had been looted and burned by Apaches. That night,
Baylor recalled, they were especially vigilant in camp. He told his
wife, "If a row comes off tonight, don't scream. Put Mary (the

youngest girl) in the oven of the cooking stove. Lie down with Kate and Helen and remain quiet." Fortunately the Apaches, seeing that they were outnumbered by Baylor's party, bypassed it. The Baylors went on through Wild Rose Pass, up Limpia Canyon and through Fort Davis, past El Muerto Springs and Van Horn Wells, where they again saw signs of Apaches, and finally reached the tree-shaded plaza of Ysleta, their destination, in safety. Twenty years later Baylor wrote an account of this trip to the "far, wild country," as he called it, for the *El Paso Herald*. By then El Paso, which had a population of several hundred when Baylor arrived, had grown into a city of sixteen thousand people.

Today El Paso has a population of eight hundred thousand. I have been replicating the western end of Baylor's trip for nearly ten years now, driving from Fort Davis to El Paso and back once every couple of months, and recently it has seemed like half of those eight hundred thousand people are out on Interstate 10 every day. It took Baylor about two weeks to get from Fort Davis to El Paso. It takes me about three hours, but it seems like most of the other folks on the interstate are trying to cut my time in half. I put the cruise control at the legal speed limit of eighty, but other drivers constantly breeze around me at ninety or even a hundred. The worst offenders are Californians, who not only hit three-digit speeds but have enormous bundles flapping in the wind on the tops of their SUVs. Like Baylor, they travel with a lot of baggage.

My earliest memory of El Paso is of changing trains there on a trip to California when I was seven, in 1947. My mother and I had an hour between trains and we spent it walking along a street near the station, looking in shop windows. One window had an entire miniature frontier town in it, populated by live white mice, who scurried in and out of the buildings on a bed of wood shavings. Something had agitated the mice just as we approached the window, and they were madly racing around the little village, ricocheting off buildings and off of each other. It made a lasting impression on my seven-year-old mind and is a perfect metaphor for El Paso today.

I find El Paso almost impossible to drive in. The city is squeezed between Mount Franklin, Fort Bliss, a huge railroad yard, and the Rio Grande, and no matter where I want to go one of these features is in the way and I get lost trying to drive around it. The streets are always full of fast-moving traffic, unlike those in Fort Davis, which are primarily used as napping spots by dogs. There are other hazards. El Paso is the violent weather capital of America. My wife and I once ran into the worst rainstorm either of us have ever encountered in our lives on Interstate 10 just east of town. It was coming down so hard and fast I could barely see the hood of our car. I managed to pull onto the shoulder and stop, but the wind was buffeting the car so hard I was sure we were going to be tipped into the ditch, which was full to overflowing. We sat there and prayed for a good half hour before the storm moved on. On another occasion, coming into El Paso from the north, we drove into a blinding rain. I thought it would be safer to get off of the interstate so I pulled onto Mesa Street, which was not only a foot deep in water but full of the boulders that had been placed down the center strip as ornamental rocks and were now tumbling down the pavement in the current. It was like driving down a Colorado trout stream in a spring flood.

I recently had to drive to El Paso and back twice in one week, first to purchase and then to pick up a new computer in Cielo Vista Mall. My compensation for the trips was two delicious lunches, one at the Café Central downtown, which I regard as the best restaurant between Dallas and Los Angeles, and the other at Tara Thai on Mesa Street. But the trips were still made nerve-wracking by the amount of traffic encountered. In between them I stopped off at the hospital in Alpine to visit Cecilia Thompson, and I ran into my friend Mojella Moore, a lady in her eighties, sitting in the waiting room. I joined her for a few minutes and told her I had just been to El Paso and had to go back, and she said, "The last time I was in El Paso was on December 23, 1991. We drove through a snowstorm on the way there and another one on the way back. I haven't been there since." Mojella is a smart woman.

February 2, 2012

✛ 46 ✛

BRYAN WOOLLEY'S
WONDERFUL ROOM

I CANNOT REMEMBER exactly when I first encountered Bryan Woolley's writing. I do remember that when I was working for the Dallas Historical Society in the late 1970s he was on the staff of the *Dallas Times Herald,* and that we met once or twice. I moved away from Texas in 1979, and a few years later Woolley moved over to the *Dallas Morning News.* Occasionally, someone would send me one of his feature stories, usually a piece of finely-honed writing about someone who did something peculiar for a living or about some odd corner of Texas. It was not until I moved to Fort Davis nine years ago that I realized Woolley was from Fort Davis; someone described a house that my wife and I were eyeing enviously as "the house that Bryan Woolley grew up in." It was then that I also realized that he had achieved heroic status in the Big Bend. People pointed out his boyhood home to strangers.

I soon found out why. I got hold of his 1977 novel, *Time and Place,* and quickly decided that it was one of the best novels about adolescence that I had ever read. The time and place in which the novel is set is Fort Davis in 1952, the year of the polio epidemic. The plot involves a young man coming to grips with the death of his best friend and with other pressures that are so painful at seventeen and so difficult for adults to write about. The place is accurately and evocatively delineated, but the plot and the characters transcend it. To say that *Time and Place* is a novel about Fort Davis is like saying that *Catcher in the Rye* is a novel about a prep school in Pennsylvania.

Woolley has written three other novels besides *Time and Place* as well as nine nonfiction works and two children's books. Now he has published a short memoir, *The Wonderful Room*. Like his Fort Davis novel, it is also about a vanished time and place.

The wonderful room of the title is the newsroom of the *El Paso Times*, where Woolley worked as a cub reporter from 1955 to 1958. In the pre-computer days of hot type, newsrooms were noisy, frantic places, with typewriters banging, telephones ringing, teletypes clicking, and reporters shouting for copy boys. Woolley catches the atmosphere perfectly, recalling not only the racket generated by the activity in the room but the vibrations of the presses in the basement. He tells what it was like for an eighteen-year-old boy, fresh out of Fort Davis High School, to become a man in that room, and the two cities, El Paso and Juarez, that were extensions of it.

Woolley's first chapter is actually about Fort Davis, where school superintendent George Roy Moore, recognizing Woolley's talent for writing, got him a job as a stringer for the *El Paso Times* when he was a junior in high school. Woolley wrote obituaries of prominent local citizens and feature stories about old-timers and mailed them off to Ted Raynor, regional news editor of the *Times*, who occasionally printed them and paid Woolley fifteen cents per column inch for the ones that were published. Woolley's mentor in Fort Davis was Barry Scobee, a retired newspaperman who was justice of the peace and county coroner and who showed Woolley how to write feature stories. Woolley remembers Scobee as the happiest man he has ever known. He didn't have much money, Woolley says, but he told Woolley, "I never saw a coffin with saddlebags."

When he graduated from high school Woolley high-tailed it to El Paso, where he talked his way into a part-time job developing photographs for the *Times*'s photographer. After being fired and re-hired a couple of times—a common experience for newspapermen in those days, Woolley says—he became a full-time reporter, and the rest of the book is about his experiences in that job. He covered the police station (and went along when the cops pulled an occasional corpse out of the Rio Grande) and interviewed visiting celebrities, including Conrad Hilton, Ty Cobb, Andres Segovia, and Louis Armstrong. He remembers Cobb as "a great and funny storyteller"; about his interview with Armstrong he says he remembers nothing "except that for fifteen minutes I was in the presence of a god" (Woolley played the trumpet in high school). He covered a strike at the ASARCO copper smelter, traded tips with a Juarez reporter who got him bullfight seats in return for movie passes in El Paso, and tried to rehabilitate a professional burglar who ended up burglarizing the bar that Woolley got him a job at—and then hit the bar owner's home on his way out of town.

All of these make good stories, but Woolley's true genius is for catching the atmosphere of a daily paper's newsroom in the 1950s. I recently read an interview with Charles Portis, author of *True Grit*, in which Portis reminisced about his experiences as a reporter for the *Arkansas Gazette* in the 1950s. One of the fixtures of the *Gazette* was a ninety-year-old copyeditor called Mr. Heiskell, who insisted that Tokyo be spelled with an *i* and refused to allow reporters to use the word "evacuate" for fear that it would remind readers of a bodily function. Mr. Heiskell sometimes speculated out loud on how different things would be if Robert E. Lee had been able to use a scouting airplane at Gettysburg. Mr. Heiskell would have been right at home in Woolley's newsroom.

The Wonderful Room is a small book, only sixty-four pages long, but it is beautifully designed and illustrated with sketches by Dean Hollingsworth, who illustrated the chapters when they originally appeared as feature stories in the *Dallas Morning News* in 2006. It is published by Bryce Milligan's Wings Press in San Antonio and sells for $10.95, and it is a bargain.

In his preface, Woolley says that his book is a memoir of the days when newspaper reporters felt that they were doing something special and essential, even holy, "that First Amendment thing," he calls it. Now, he says, the few remaining daily papers are corporate products, tailored to what will sell to consumers. "I'm afraid our democracy is in big trouble," he concludes.

He's right. We need more reporters like Bryan Woolley.

February 17, 2011

✥ 47 ✥

AUSTIN 1962,
FORT DAVIS 2011

DURING THE SUMMER of 1962, I lived in a small garage apartment behind a big house on Nueces Street in Austin. I was ostensibly taking a crash course in German at the University of Texas so that I could pass the German translation exam then required of all PhD candidates. My next-door neighbors up the alley were a group of people my age who inhabited a much larger garage apartment, a warren of rooms and staircases that everyone called the Ghetto. Its residents that summer included Janis Joplin, Powell St. John, Lanny and Ramsey Wiggins, John Clay, Tary Owens, Wally Stopher and his brother Tommy, and Tommy's girlfriend, Olga, and several other people who came and went. Most of them were musical. Joplin, St. John, and Lanny Wiggins had a band called the Waller Creek Boys that played at a nearby bar, Threadgill's Filling Station; John Clay played the banjo and wrote songs about the small West Texas town he grew up in. Some of the Ghettoites later moved to San Francisco and had professional recording careers. Powell St. John formed a band called Mother Earth which cut several albums with Tracy Nelson, and he is still writing songs. Janis Joplin, of course, skyrocketed to fame after the 1967 Monterey Pop Festival. But that summer no one was famous or even thought about being famous. We just thought about having a good time.

Part of our good time was Friday night fish fries at the Ghetto. One of the residents was a fellow named Don Kleen, who loved to fish. On Friday mornings he would take a cane pole, hike down to a spot on the Colorado River called Deep Eddy, and fish all day. In the evening, we would gather under the huge shade trees in the packed-earth yard of the Ghetto and eat what Dan caught, washed down with cold beer. The Waller Creek Boys would get out their instruments—Joplin played the autoharp at the time. John Clay would pick up his banjo, and we would all sit back under the trees and listen to the music, singing along on the choruses. Clay had two songs he would render in a high, whining voice: "On the Road to Mingus," about a fatal drag race between Mingus and Strawn; and another one about a woman named Brenda whose husband ran around. We never tired of hearing them. One night Joplin sang Woody Guthrie's "Roll On, Columbia" so loudly that the police came. It was an idyllic summer that changed the direction of my life. Among other things I never learned German, and I never went back to graduate school.

I was reminded of that summer one evening last spring when Todd Jagger organized what he called a house party at the Cow Camp in Fort Davis. In spite of its primitive-sounding name, the Cow Camp is a large and elegant home on Court Street in Fort Davis, originally built in 1883 by rancher Samuel A. Thompson and now owned by Mark and Irene Fillman. One of the best features of the Cow Camp is a big tree-shaded backyard with a concrete slab and a small stage, and this is where the house party took place. The featured performer was Bob Livingston, founder of the Lost Gonzo Band, which backed up both Michael Martin Murphey and Jerry Jeff Walker. My wife and I and our houseguests got there to find about two dozen people sitting under the trees, sipping cold beer and listening to Livingston singing "London Homesick Blues" and "Up Against the Wall, Redneck Mother," and a dozen other songs from the 1970s.

Livingston is a consummate performer and he put his best into every song, even though the audience was small. He talked a little between songs, and at one point he told how Ray Wiley Hubbard came to write "Up Against the Wall, Redneck Mother." He said that in the early 1970s he and some other musicians were visiting Hubbard at his cabin outside of Red River, New Mexico, and they ran out of beer. Hubbard volunteered to go to a bar in town and get a case. In the bar he was confronted by a woman in her fifties who taunted him about his long hair and leather pants and called him a Communist. He was trying to extricate himself from the situation when the woman's son came up from behind and hit him, knocking him down. Somehow he got out of the place with his case of beer, and when he got back to the cabin he told his friends what had happened by writing the song. It was recorded by Jerry Jeff Walker in 1973 and became an immediate hit.

My wife and I were delighted to hear this story because we have always had a soft spot for that song. When we lived in Washington, DC, we always attended the Texas State Society's Black Tie and Boots Inaugural Ball, held every four years. It was the best of all the inaugural balls, strictly nonpartisan, with superb entertainment direct from Texas. The 1989 ball honored George H. W. Bush, and we arrived to find about three thousand people crammed into one of four adjoining ballrooms at the Washington Hilton, awaiting the arrival of the new president and his wife. The first person we saw was Molly Ivins, who said, "Let's get out of here. Jerry Jeff Walker is playing his heart out to about twenty people in the next room." We followed Molly into the next room, and sure enough there was Jerry Jeff, surrounded by a very small group of Texans, including a sextet of bejeweled and beautifully coiffed Midland matrons in evening gowns. They had Petroleum Club Republican written all over them, but when Jerry Jeff broke into "Up Against the Wall" they joined right in. My wife, who had never lived in Texas, was open-mouth astonished. "They know all the words," she said.

Last spring's house party was the first in what Todd Jagger says he hopes will be a series, built around the visits of musicians to the

Big Bend. "It would be nice to do one a month," he told me. I completely agree. I would enjoy revisiting Austin in the summer of '62 on a regular basis.

August 25, 2011

✦ 48 ✦

A KILLING IN THE BIG BEND

OLD TROUBLES in the Big Bend are like the pearl in the oyster. The simple fact of a man's being killed in a dispute is the irritating grain of sand; then layers of narrative build up around it until the story is a polished pearl, handed down from generation to generation as a community treasure, even though it has its beginning in tragedy.

Most of the killings in the Big Bend in the early days were the result of the way the range cattle industry was organized and the fact that most of the people involved in it were Southerners. Southerners had a heightened sense of personal honor. A nineteenth-century visitor to the South wrote, "Call a Yankee a liar and he'll say 'you're another'; call a Southerner a liar and he'll kill you." In the Big Bend's open range ranching system, herds of cattle belonging to different owners grazed on enormous tracts of unfenced public land. They mixed together, and when it came time to sort them out, there was plenty of room for disputes about who owned what and plenty of occasions for men to call each other liars. The killing of Jim McCutcheon by Dick Riggs in 1906 was the result of just such a dispute.

I first heard the story from Wid McCutcheon of Fort Davis, a great-grandson of Jim McCutcheon's brother Willis and a former sheriff of Jeff Davis County. Several years ago, Wid took me on a tour of the country north of Fort Davis where the McCutcheons ranched a hundred years ago and told me stories about the places that we passed. He explained that four McCutcheon brothers, Willis, Bill, Jim, and Beau, came into that country in the 1880s from South Texas and acquired ranches around Barilla Springs, Cavalry Springs, and Seven Springs. At one time they controlled most of the northern part of Jeff Davis County. All of the brothers had hot tempers and a penchant for quarrels. In 1891, Wid said, Bill McCutcheon got into an argument with some freighters whose burros had gotten into the alfalfa on his Seven Springs ranch. He started shooting the burros; the freighters shot back, and Bill McCutcheon was killed. No one was ever indicted for his murder.

Wid's narrative of Jim McCutcheon's death was equally straightforward. In 1906 there was a roundup at Barilla Springs. Dick Riggs had recently sold a ranch there to Jim McCutcheon, and he and McCutcheon got into an argument over the ownership of some of the cattle, which Riggs said belonged to his wife and were not included in the sale. McCutcheon started hitting Riggs over the head with a quirt, and Riggs drew a pistol and fatally shot McCutcheon. When he realized what he had done, Riggs spurred his horse, rode into Alpine, and gave himself up to the Texas Ranger there. He was tried in El Paso for murder a year later and acquitted on grounds of self defense. Wid finished the story by saying that after the trial, Riggs went to New Mexico. Shortly afterward, Jim McCutcheon's two brothers also went to New Mexico. They came back, Wid said, but Riggs didn't.

There are other tellings of this story, embellished with more and sometimes contradictory details. Roy Reid, who came into the Barilla Springs country in 1909 and knew the surviving McCutcheon brothers, related a more complicated version of the matter to his young friend Winfield Russell McAfee, who published it in his book *The Cattlemen* (Alvin, Texas: Davis Mountains Press, 1992). According to Reid, a man named Miller owned a section of land with a spring on it near Jim McCutcheon's headquarters. In the summer of 1906, Miller leased the grazing and watering rights on his section to Jim

McCutcheon for a hundred dollars. A few days later he leased the same rights to Dick Riggs for two hundred dollars. Riggs rounded up his cattle to move them to the newly leased land; McCutcheon showed up at the roundup and asked Riggs where he was moving the cattle to, and the argument ensued. According to Reid, Riggs shot McCutcheon twice. The first shot knocked McCutcheon off his horse and broke the quirt-wielding arm. The second shot, the fatal one, was fired when McCutcheon was on the ground and reaching for his pistol with his good arm. The bullet broke that arm and entered his stomach.

Reid also added another detail to the story. He said that when Dick Riggs took off for Alpine, a deputy sheriff named Stuckler, who was at the roundup, shouted, "I deputize everybody at this roundup to catch that man." Riggs's brother, Monroe Riggs, pulled his rifle from its scabbard, slid off his horse, and said, "I'll kill the first man who starts after him." No one moved.

Lucy Jacobson and Mildred Nored also tell about the shooting in their book, *Jeff Davis County, Texas.* They add an account of Dick Riggs's trial for murder in El Paso in 1907, which explains his acquittal. The state's attorney was arguing that Jim McCutcheon was unarmed when he was killed, and had produced witnesses to testify to that. Riggs's attorney argued that McCutcheon was armed, and that Riggs shot him in self defense, fearing for his life. In cross-questioning Jim McElroy, the McCutcheon foreman and one of the state's witnesses, Riggs's attorney asked him a series of rapid-fire questions and suddenly said, "Mr. McElroy, what did you do with Mr. McCutcheon's gun when you picked it up?" McElroy, caught off guard, said, "I stuck it in my boot." That convinced the jury of Riggs's innocence.

A friend of mine in Alpine who is a great-niece of Dick Riggs assures me that Riggs was not killed in New Mexico by the McCutcheon brothers but moved to Kerrville after his trial and lived there for many years, respected and well liked.

One thing about the story is certain. Jim McCutcheon died on the kitchen table of the U Bar ranch, where his friends had taken him on horseback. They sent for a doctor, who drove from Pecos in a buggy but arrived too late to save him. McCutcheon was forty-six years old. He died a victim of Southern pride and a hot temper.

August 4, 2011

✤ 49 ✤

MARFA'S FORT D. A. RUSSELL

A FEW MILES SOUTH of Washington, DC, on the Maryland side of the Potomac River, is an imposing stone fortress called Fort Washington. It was built in 1824 so that the British fleet could never again sail up the Potomac and menace the national capital, as it had in 1814 when the British burned the city. Its construction was a classic case of locking the stable after the horse is gone.

The same thing could be said of Fort D. A. Russell at Marfa, now the home of the Chinati Foundation. Fort D. A. Russell started out in 1911 as Camp Marfa, a scattering of tents in a pasture south of the railroad tracks in Marfa, the temporary base of two troops (about one hundred men) of the Third US Cavalry. The cavalrymen were sent to the Big Bend from Fort Sam Houston in San Antonio to try to control the arms smuggling into Mexico that had reached epidemic proportions with the outbreak of the Madero revolution against the government of Porfirio Diaz the year before. The arms smuggling was a violation of federal law, and, as the Border Patrol had not yet been established, the army was the only enforcement agent the government had.

The cavalry spent five futile years in the Big Bend, trying to intercept smugglers with about as much success as the Border Patrol now has in turning back illegal immigrants. Then, in 1916, the army's mission changed dramatically. On May 5 of that year, sixty armed men crossed the Rio Grande from Mexico and attacked the little communities of Glen Springs and Boquillas, Texas, both now in Big Bend National Park. They looted the stores

✤ 193

at both places and killed three US army soldiers and a seven-year-old boy at Glen Springs. At Boquillas they kidnapped the storekeeper and his assistant and took them into Mexico with them.

In response to the raid, President Wilson ordered the National Guard of four states to the Big Bend, and Camp Marfa suddenly became the headquarters for a major military operation. A dozen army subposts were established along the Rio Grande, all of which were supplied by wagon train and pack mules from Camp Marfa. The Sixth United States Cavalry established its regimental headquarters there. The soldiers and their horses remained under tents, but the tents covered a lot of ground. The raids continued through 1917 and 1918, and several punitive cavalry expeditions into Mexico were launched from Camp Marfa.

In November 1918, World War I ended. The army had a huge appropriation for fiscal year 1918-1919, and another for 1919-1920. It seemed sensible to use some of it to improve the army facilities along the Mexican border. Between 1919 and 1921, 184 permanent structures went up at Camp Marfa—barracks, officers' quarters, stables, blacksmith and machine shops, a theater, an officers' club, a gymnasium. Buildings also replaced tents at the subposts along the river, and a stone fort was erected in Vieja Pass. The army was now ready for any raiders who dared to cross the Rio Grande.

But 1920 was also the year that Mexico achieved some degree of political stability under President Álvaro Obregón, the one-armed general who overthrew Venustiano Carranza in 1919. The raids stopped and never resumed. The cavalry settled into a somnolent and pleasant existence at Camp Marfa, pumping about half a million dollars a year into the local economy and providing a stream of bachelor officers to serve as escorts and, in some cases, husbands for ranchers' daughters. Marfa became an army town. The cavalry officers, many of whom had served in the Philippines, Cuba, and Europe, elevated the tone of local society. There were dances at the officers' club and the Paisano Hotel, and polo match-es on Wednesday and Sunday afternoons, followed by polo teas at the officers' club. In 1930, the year that Camp Marfa was promot-ed to a fort and renamed Fort D. A. Russell, a First Cavalry polo team went to Mexico City on a special train to play a series of matches against a Mexican army team, taking a group of promi-nent Marfans and their wives with them. The Mexican team played return matches in Marfa, bringing along a sixty-piece brass band which played for a series of dances at the Paisano Hotel in the evenings.

Fort D. A. Russell kept Marfa afloat during the first years of the Depression, but early in 1932 the axe fell. The Hoover administra-tion announced that as an economy measure the army would close fifty-three military posts and Marfa's fort was on that list. Texas's congressional delegation swung into action to save it, but to no avail. As a last-ditch effort, Marfa rancher Luke Brite, whose ranch had been raided in 1917, went to Washington to plead with his fellow rancher, Vice President-elect John Nance Garner of Uvalde. Garner listened sympathetically and sent Brite to see General Douglas MacArthur, the army chief of staff. MacArthur told Brite that not only was Fort D. A. Russell redundant, the cav-alry itself was redundant. The days of border raids were over, MacArthur said, and if they ever resumed, airplanes from Fort Sam Houston in San Antonio could reach the Big Bend in three hours. He told Brite that the fort would close on January 1, 1933, and the First Cavalry would be shipped off to Fort Knox, Kentucky, where they would learn to drive tanks. That was exactly what happened. The First Cavalry held a final mounted review on December 14. One horse, Louie, too old at thirty-one to be of fur-ther use to the army, was draped in black, shot, and buried on the grounds, a symbol of the regiment's demise as a mounted unit. The regiment's other horses were sent to other cavalry regiments in Texas. The men of the First Cavalry left Marfa in a convoy of eighty-four trucks on January 2, 1933, and the gates of Fort D. A. Russell were locked behind them.

As things turned out, the growing threat of war in Europe brought about the reopening of the fort in July 1935, but it was reopened as a mechanized field-artillery training base, and the clop of horses' hooves was seldom heard on its parade ground.

This year Alpine is celebrating the centennial of aviation in the Big Bend, and Fort Davis is celebrating the centennial of its courthouse, jail, and bank. Marfa should be celebrating the centennial of Fort D. A. Russell.

May 5, 2011

✣ 50 ✣

THE RONQUILLO GRANT

SOME ASPECTS of Texas history can best be understood in terms of the deeply rooted human tendency to believe that all land acquired cheaply will inevitably increase in value. Nothing so well illustrates this as the story of the Ronquillo Grant, a chimera that shimmered over a large portion of the Big Bend for fifty years, enriching several middlemen and, in the end, leaving a Chicago millionaire nearly five million dollars poorer.

The story begins in Presidio del Norte (now Ojinaga) in the late 1840s, when Ben Leaton, an Anglo-American trader and the builder of Fort Leaton, now a Texas state historical site, persuaded Cesario Herrera, the *alcalde* of Presidio del Norte, to forge some land titles for him. For a cash consideration, Herrera obligingly produced some backdated documents that allowed Leaton to dispossess the farmers who were cultivating land on the Texas side of the river near Fort Leaton that Leaton had immediate use for. Then, with an eye to the future, he got Herrera to forge a grant of 225 leagues of land (about one million acres) lying in what is now Brewster, Presidio, and Jeff Davis Counties. The grant was backdated to 1832 and was purportedly made by Herrera as *alcalde* to a Mexican army captain, José Ygnacio Ronquillo, who had been living at Presidio del Norte. Herrera also forged field notes for a survey of the grant and a chain of title that involved transfers of the grant from Ronquillo to Hipólito Acosta and from Acosta to Juana Pedraza, Leaton's common-law wife. Herrera and Leaton were careful to ensure that all of the names of the people in the forged documents, except that of Juana Pedraza, were those of people who were dead.

Leaton intended to have his million-acre grant confirmed by the Texas legislature, but he died before he could complete the process, and his heirs failed to follow through on it. The land within its alleged boundaries was treated as public land by the state of Texas, and was granted to railroads or sold to individuals. Everyone forgot about the Ronquillo Grant until 1883, when silver was discovered at Shafter. Leaton's grandson, Victor Ochoa, a man worth a book to himself, revived his family's claim. He hired Trevanion Teel, a flamboyant San Antonio lawyer who once won a murder case by swallowing the indictment and then challenging the state's attorney to produce it, to sue the mining company for a million dollars plus $6,000 a month rent. While Teel was preparing his case another claimant appeared, a Juarez attorney named Estanislado Ronquillo, who said that he was the grandson of Captain José Ygnacio Ronquillo and thus the legitimate heir to the grant. Teel was able to prove in court that while attorney Ronquillo's grandfather was indeed named José Ygnacio Ronquillo, he had never been a captain in the Mexican army and had never lived at Presidio and therefore was not the man to whom the grant had allegedly been made. Before that happened, however, the faux descendant had sold his claim to James J. Fitzgerrell of Las Vegas, New Mexico, for $100,000. Fitzgerrell in turn sold two-thirds of his interest to Seth Crews of Chicago for $150,000, and then Crews and Fitzgerrell jointly sold the whole grant to Ernest Dale Owen of Chicago for the incredible sum of $4,500,000.

Owen also bought Victor Ochoa's claim, which got Teel out of the way, and in 1892 filed suit against the silver miners, the Presidio Mining Company. In preparing his brief, he got involved in a web of further forgeries which is much too complicated to go into here. The case ended up in the Fifth Circuit Court of Appeals in New Orleans, and the testimony given there provides interesting insights into conditions around Fort Leaton in 1850. Depositions were taken from everyone still living in Presidio who knew Leaton, Juana Pedraza, and Cesario Herrera, and they all emerge as unprincipled scoundrels of the first water. Witnesses testified that the alleged grant was far larger than provided for in Mexican law, that it was beyond the power of an *alcalde* to make such land grants, that even if it were a legitimate grant Ronquillo would not have been legally permitted to transfer it so soon after receiving it, and finally, that the documents supporting it were palpable fakes. The Ronquillo Grant faded away, leaving Robert Dale Owen holding a four-and-a-half-million-dollar bag. The moral of the whole sorry tale is that it is possible to make money out of land in the Big Bend if you can find the right sucker before the bottom drops out of the deal.

March 25, 2004

✣ 51 ✣

THE FOOD SHARK

TWENTY-FIVE YEARS AGO
the Irish novelist Roddy Doyle
published a hilarious book called *The Van* about the misadventures of three working-class Dubliners who purchase an old van and try to sell fish and chips from it. In Doyle's novel, everything goes wrong that possibly can, and the entrepreneurs end up driving the van into the Irish Sea and leaving it there. I doubt if this will be the fate of Marfa's food van, the Food Shark. I spent an afternoon not long ago talking with the Food Shark's proprietors, Adam Bork and Krista Steinhauer, and they seem far more competent than Doyle's characters, who are lovable but seldom sober. Another major difference is that Doyle's trio started their mobile food business out of economic necessity, while Bork and Steinhauer started theirs because they bought a van and then had to figure out what to do with it.

The van is not exactly a thing of beauty or an example of classic automobile design. It consists of a bulky aluminum body built thirty or so years ago onto a 1974 Ford truck chassis by a now defunct outfit in San Angelo called Ford Brothers. Internal evidence shows that it was once a Rainbow Bread delivery truck, but when Bork and Steinhauer spotted it sitting behind a short-lived barbecue joint in Marfa last year it had been converted into a food service vehicle. "It had a lot of personality," Steinhauer told me, "a kind of cute grill and face." They decided that they couldn't live without it, and with the help of their friend Ginger Griffice they bought it (Griffice, who sometimes helps out with lunch at the Food Shark, describes herself as a "plankholder" in the enterprise, which must be something more substantial than a stake-holder).

When they bought the van in February 2006, neither Bork nor Steinhauer, who came to Marfa from Austin in 2004 to help open the Thunderbird Motel, had any previous experience in the food-preparation business, although Bork was once a waiter and busboy in an Austin restaurant and Steinhauer had put in a brief stint as a cheese and chocolate buyer for a specialty food store in San Francisco. In fact, Bork was a well-known musician in Austin, play-ing the electric guitar in venues like Antone's and the Continental Club under the name Earth Pig (he will be putting out an album soon, recorded at the Gory Smelley studio in Marfa).

Steinhauer, however, lived in Florence, Italy, for four years and traveled a good deal in the Eastern Mediterranean, where she acquired a taste for what she describes as "Middle Eastern street food." Not only that, her father had once been in the food van business, and when she told him about the new vehicle he started sending her drawings showing how to install kitchen equipment in it (actually, when she first sent him a picture of the van, his response was, "Maybe you should have sent me a photo before you bought it," but then the drawings started arriving). "Things just jelled," Bork says. "It was just crazy enough to work."

They started serving lunch from the van in October 2006. Steinhauer is in charge of the menus, which have a core of Middle Eastern falafel and hummus supplemented with daily specials that tend toward dishes that Steinhauer describes as "more instantly recognizable," such as barbecue sandwiches and tacos. She pre-pares most of the food, while Bork is in charge of mixing the hum-mus and taking care of the cold drinks. Their day starts about 7:00 a.m., when Steinhauer starts making the day's supply of falafel in her catering kitchen and transferring it to the van for final assem-bly. Falafel, she explained, is a mixture of ground garbanzo beans, cilantro, Italian parsley, fresh mint, garlic, and onions, "plus a couple of little secrets." The van is equipped with an icebox, a hot plate, and a deep fryer, and the falafel balls that are the Food Shark's staple are formed from Steinhauer's premixed supply and fried when the customer orders them. Hummus is also based on garbanzo beans, cooked and mixed with lemon juice and olive oil—"We go through buckets of olive oil," Steinhauer said. Bork and Steinhauer obtain their ingredients from a variety of sources. A wholesale food company provides the basics, but they make monthly runs to Austin and El Paso for cheese and olive oil, and they are making increasing use of locally grown cucumbers, carrots, herbs, and greens. "The more we can get locally the better," Steinhauer says.

By 11:30 a.m. on most days, the van is in place next to the railroad crossing on South Highland Avenue. They generally serve lunch four days a week, but as Bork says, "Like all Marfa businesses that is not an absolute." On open days between fifty and eighty people will have lunch at tables under a metal canopy provided by Tim Crowley, who owns the land that the van parks on and has been a major supporter of the enterprise. Diners are treated to classic country music—Ray Price and Tammy Wynette, with an occasional sprinkling of rock bands like The Guess Who—played at a moderate volume from a pair of orange speakers mounted on top of the van. One of the first things Bork added after buying the vehicle was an eight-track tape sound system. After all, he is a musician. They usually serve their last meal about 2:30—"unless we run out of food," Bork cautions—and by 3:00 p.m. the van is buttoned down and ready to be driven back to the catering kitchen. Bork says that they put 1.2 miles a day on it, and have not yet had to change the oil.

I asked the question that must be on the tip of everybody's tongue the first time they talk to Bork and Steinhauer: why do they call their van the Food Shark? The name causes a certain amount of confusion with non-English speaking visitors to Marfa, who occasionally step up to the window and want to know what kind of shark is being served. Bork says that the name just popped into his head. "It might have something to do with the way the truck looks," he says. I'm not sure what this says about someone who occasionally calls himself Earth Pig, but wherever it came from, Food Shark has become synonymous with good food in Marfa.

August 23, 2007

THE HIGHLAND HEREFORD
ROUGH RIDERS

EVERY AMERICAN has heard of Teddy Roosevelt's Rough Riders, the volunteer cavalry unit that Roosevelt and Colonel Leonard Wood took to Cuba in the Spanish-American War, but how many people have heard of the Highland Hereford Rough Riders? I certainly had not, until I started reading old issues of the *Big Bend Sentinel* in the Marfa Public Library in connection with some other research that I was doing.

The Highland Hereford Rough Riders grew out of the days of panic, confusion, and anger that followed the Japanese attack on Pearl Harbor on December 7, 1941. Oddly enough, the *Big Bend Sentinel* of December 12, 1941 (the paper came out on Fridays then), does not even mention the attack or the war; the big story on the front page is about an upcoming Rotary Club meeting.

I suppose by then everyone knew what had happened, and there was enough local news to fill up the paper. However, the next issue, December 19, is full of stories about emergency preparations at Fort D. A. Russell, a planned blackout practice, sales of Defense Bonds, ladies flocking to join the Presidio County Red Cross, and a report on a Marfa man who sustained injuries when the Japanese bombed Clark Field in the Philippines. Buried on page four is a story about the Rotary Club meeting mentioned in the previous week's paper. It seems that at the meeting, which took place on December 16, rancher George Jones proposed the organization of a home defense unit composed of "men who ride horses and shoot rifles."

The unit, Jones explained, should include at least one hundred horsemen and a back-up force of pickup truck drivers who would trailer the horses to points where they would be needed. Another member, W. B. DeVolin, was quoted as saying, "This is a cavalry country, not one for infantry." The club president, Albert Logan, chimed in that "A man on a horse was of much more value in this country." Jones threw in an added advantage: if the unit were organized quickly, he said, it could participate in the Sun Carnival parade in El Paso. After this discussion, the members patiently listened to a book review of Dorothy Thomson's *Political Guide*, but it is clear they left the meeting ready to join the cavalry.

The Friday evening after the Rotary Club meeting, December 19, there was a mass meeting at the Marfa City Hall to discuss defense measures. Most of the talk amounted to instructions from Lieutenant Colonel Bertram Frankenberger, the commander of Fort D. A. Russell, about how to organize blackouts if Japanese planes should appear over Marfa, but R. I. Bledsoe also announced that a home defense cavalry unit was being formed to counter the threat of Axis saboteurs slipping across the border. Of course, this was less than twenty-five years after the border raids during the Mexican Revolution, and the vulnerability of the border was on everyone's mind.

The next Friday afternoon, December 26, seventy-four ranchers gathered in Marfa. George Jones opened the meeting with a speech saying that the unit was being organized "not just for getting publicity" but for serious business, and if people joined they had better be ready to saddle up and head out at any time. Everyone present was asked to step forward and sign a register listing the equipment they could contribute to the unit—horses, saddles, guns, pickup trucks, and trailers. The *Big Bend Sentinel* listed the names of those who registered. They included every prominent cattleman in Presidio, Brewster, and Jeff Davis Counties.

Shortly afterward the annual meeting of the Highland

Hereford Breeders Association, a group formed in 1918 to market Hereford cattle raised in the Big Bend, was held in Marfa. Virtually all of the men who had signed up for the cavalry unit were members of the association, and at the association meeting George Jones announced that the new unit would be called the Highland Hereford Rough Riders. He also announced that Governor Coke Stevenson and Brigadier General J. Watt Page, the adjutant general of Texas, had approved the unit and that it would have the legal status of a county home-guard unit, subject to the orders of the sheriffs of the three counties it would serve. Most of the members were well above draft age.

The apogee of the Highland Hereford Rough Riders came on Saturday, January 24, when the members assembled at the Bloys Camp Meeting Grounds for a formal swearing in and review. General Page was there with his staff, and so was the Mexican general in command of the Juarez garrison and his staff. In spite of George Jones's insistence that publicity was not the organization's goal, cameraman Jimmy Lederer of Universal Newsreels turned up to film the proceedings so the rest of America in their local movie theatres could view the ranchmen's regiment assembling. John Stroud, an entertainer and banquet speaker from Amarillo who impersonated the rustic character "Old Whiz," supposed foreman of the Frying Pan Ranch, was on hand. The Highland Hereford volunteers galloped past Lederer's camera in columns of fours and flourished their rifles, then dismounted and stepped smartly up to a table to sign the regimental roll. There were speeches, and everyone sat down to a barbecue dinner prepared by Hayes Mitchell, Frank Jones, and B. H. Davis from donated beef.

Ted Harper, who at ninety-four may be the only surviving member of the Highland Hereford Rough Riders, was there that day. He remembers it vividly, and told me, "We had our horses and our guns and we were ready if they needed us. The country was pretty wide awake—we didn't know what to expect."

By February 1942, it became evident that the first stages of the war were going to be fought in the Pacific and not in the Big Bend. As a consequence, the Rough Riders seem to have faded away; at least, there is no more mention of them in the newspaper. A Texas Home Defense Company was organized in Marfa in March, but they were infantry. The Highland Hereford Breeders Association is still around, of course. There are a lot of cattlemen's associations in the Southwest, but I'll bet they are the only one that ever had its own cavalry unit.

July 22, 2010

✜ 53 ✜

THE ROAD TO THE MINE

HISTORIANS use many gateways to enter the past. Some study treaties and diplomatic history; some wars and military history; some, agriculture and trade and the evolution of settlement. Some even study the development of roads and highways. This past month I joined that last group and spent a good deal of time in the Marfa courthouse looking into the history of roads in Presidio County, and it has given me a totally new perspective on the history of the Big Bend.

The Mother Road of the Big Bend was the Chihuahua Trail, the wagon road from San Antonio to Chihuahua City that wound from water hole to water hole across West Texas until it turned southward at Burgess Water Hole (now Kokernot Park in Alpine) and followed the course of Alamito Creek to Presidio del Norte (now Ojinaga) on the Rio Grande. That road was laid out by American merchants in Chihuahua City in 1839, and the segment of it that ran down the valley of Alamito Creek eventually became the main road from Marfa to Presidio. That segment is now the Casa Piedra Road. Most of the other roads in Presidio County's road network originally branched off from it.

The road that I have been spending most of my time on is one of those branches. When it was built in 1900, it was called the Marfa-Terlingua Freight Road, and it was the longest and most expensive road built to that date in Presidio County. It left the Marfa-Presidio road about halfway to Presidio and wound eastward across the desert past San Jacinto Mountain, then turned south across Bandera Mesa and the western edge of the Solitario and down into and through Fresno Canyon. At the mouth of Fresno Canyon it turned east again and ended at the Marfa and Mariposa Mining Company's mercury mine, about eight miles west of Terlingua. It was sixty miles long and it cost $1877.50 to build. Its only purpose was to serve the mine, which was owned by Presidio County ranchers James Normand, Tom Goldby, and Montroyd Sharp.

The Presidio County Commissioners' Court minutes reveal that when the road was built James Normand was the county commissioner from Precinct 2, and he persuaded the County Commission to appropriate $1557.50 in county funds for its construction. This was supplemented by $320.00 in private subscription, probably from the mining company. The contract for construction went to Tom Goldby. I am not implying that there was any hanky-panky involved; that was just the way things were done in those days. People ran for county commissioner to look out for their own interests.

In 1900, the largest mercantile store in Marfa was Murphy and Walker, which occupied most of the city block where Livingston's is now. Murphy and Walker supplied the Marfa and Mariposa mine with groceries, hardware, merchandise for the mine's commissary, mining machinery, and whatever else was needed, and they received the heavy flasks of mercury that were shipped back to be loaded on the railroad. Everything destined for the mine, and the mercury flasks, moved along the Marfa-Terlingua Freight Road in heavy Studebaker wagons designed to carry eight thousand pounds of freight each. The wagons were drawn by teams of six and sometimes twelve mules, harnessed two abreast at the wagon tongue and four abreast in front. The drivers rode on the mule nearest the left-hand wheel and operated the wagon's brake with a rope, one end of which was tied to the top of the brake handle; the other end was tied around the driver's saddle horn. The brake handle was counterweighted with a heavy piece of iron tied to it. The iron dragged in the road behind the wagon, leaving a trail in the dust. Unkind people said the trail was used by the freighters to find their way back to Marfa from the mine.

The heavily loaded wagons moved very slowly, usually taking about eight days to make the hundred-mile trip from Marfa to the mine, with the drivers camping out overnight along the road. A waybill in the Archives of the Big Bend for a wagonload of goods shipped to the mine from Murphy and Walker bears a sarcastic notation from whoever received the shipment. "Team galloped in at noon dead beat—96 miles in 96 hours." If you have ever been down the road in Fresno Canyon you would be surprised that they made it at all.

There was also a stage connection between the mine and Marfa. The stage was actually a two-seater mule-drawn buggy, called a hack, that carried passengers and mail to the mine and back three times a week, leaving Marfa at 7:00 a.m. and reaching the mine the evening of the next day. C. A. Hawley, an ex-school-teacher employed by the mine as an accountant, made his first trip down the Marfa-Terlingua Freight Road in it in 1905. He noticed that both the driver and the other passenger were carrying pistols and rifles, and he asked if they were expecting trouble along the way. "Oh, no," his fellow passenger replied. "It's just the custom of the country." In his memoir, *Life Along the Border*, Hawley says that the stage stopped for the night at an adobe house a few miles north of the entrance to Fresno Canyon. There the passengers were given dinner, a place to sleep, and breakfast. They did not have an opportunity to bathe, even though they were covered with dust.

A couple of weeks ago, I visited that adobe house with B. C. Bennett, who grew up in it. The Marfa-Terlingua Freight Road still leads to Bennett's Bandera Ranch, but it is impassable beyond that point. The Marfa and Mariposa Mine closed down in 1907, and there has been little traffic on the road since then, although the county now maintains it as far as the locked gate at the Big Bend Ranch State Park boundary. Standing in front of that little house, gazing across the desert toward the spire of San Jacinto Mountain a dozen miles away, it was difficult to believe that the Marfa-Terlingua Freight Road was ever a vital link to anywhere, much less to a mine from which thousands of flasks of mercury were once shipped to Marfa.

June 17, 2010

✣ 54 ✣

THE SECRET HISTORY
OF THE BIG BEND

T HE BIG BEND has two histories. There is the official his-
tory, enshrined in books like Carlysle Gram Raht's *Romance of the
Davis Mountains and Big Bend Country*; Clifford Casey's *Mirages,
Mysteries, and Reality: Brewster County, Texas*; Ron Tyler's *The
Big Bend: A History of the Last Texas Frontier*, and Cecilia
Thompson's two-volume *History of Marfa and Presidio County*,
which has just been reprinted and of which a third volume is in
the works. These excellent books all make use of the written and
published sources available to historians—official reports, public
records, newspapers, and the memoirs of early settlers—to tell the
story of the settlement and development of the Big Bend by Anglo-
Americans. It is a story that has been repeated all over the West, a
story of ranchers, railroads, town building, and community institutions like churches, schools, fraternal organizations, and women's
clubs. It is seldom a story of conflict, except for conflict with
Native Americans in the early days of settlement and conflict with
nature. In fact, one of the earlier histories of the Big Bend, by Alice
Shipman, is called *Taming the Big Bend*.

But there is another history of the Big Bend that I like to think
of as its secret history. This is the history of the Spanish-speaking
people who started coming here from Mexico at about the same
time that the first Anglo ranchers arrived and whose numbers
increased after the Mexican Revolution of 1910. They, too, built
communities and institutions, and they often came into conflict
with Anglo settlers, but their story is seldom found in the same eas-

ily accessible sources as that of the Anglo-Americans, so it has been largely omitted from even the best published histories. It remains a secret history, known only to the descendants of those who lived it.

Here is an example. Virtually every published history of the Big Bend talks about John Davis, a pioneer Anglo settler from North Carolina who settled on Alamito Creek about 1865, built a fortified adobe house there, and returned to North Carolina in 1890. Today a Texas State Historical Marker marks the site of his home. Victoriano Hernandez arrived from Mexico about 1865 and also built a fortified house on Alamito Creek, just a few miles south of Davis's. The 1870 census of Presidio County lists Hernandez as a "ranchero" with personal property valued at $4,000, making him one of the wealthiest men in the county. He died in 1903, leaving many descendants. He served for many years as a road supervisor and Presidio County election judge and was far more influential than John Davis, but his house is unmarked and there is only a brief mention of him in one of the histories of the Big Bend.

There are several stories about Victoriano Hernandez, passed down in his family, part of the secret history, that make me want to know more about him. Here is one: when he was seventy, he decided to add a chapel to his house. He ordered a large crucifix from a carver in Ojinaga, and when it was ready, Hernandez and his sons rode horseback to Ojinaga to get it. Hernandez carried it home on foot, escorted by his sons. He made the twenty-three-mile walk in one day.

During the past decade, the secret history has slowly started coming to light. In 2008, Juan Manuel Casas published *Federico Villalba's Texas*, an account of his great-grandfather's adventures as a Mexican-born rancher in the Big Bend in the 1880s and '90s and of his children's lives here. Casas based his text on a mixture of documentary evidence and family stories, with the result that some of his statements concerning the Villalba landholdings do not quite square up with the county deed records. There is plenty of conflict in the book. In 1923, one of Villalba's sons killed two Anglo men who came to his house drunk and armed, shouting racial epithets; eight years later, another son was murdered by an Anglo who was never indicted. There is a tinge of bitterness to Casas's book, and it rubbed some people the wrong way because it expressed a point of view at variance with the accepted one.

Now Armando Vasquez of Marfa has brought more of the secret history into print by publishing a memoir of his long life under the title *I Well Remember*. Vasquez was born in 1925 into a family much like the Villalbas; his grandfather Natividad Vasquez came from Mexico in 1883 and acquired land at Casa Piedra. Vasquez grew up on the family ranch there, surrounded by relatives. He writes about riding a burro to school, about doing ranch chores and helping his father in the family's store. He recalls relatives observing the moon rules for planting, cutting wood, and even conceiving children, and he mentions neighbors who observed the feast of San Isidro by carrying the saint's image in procession through their fields and brewing *tesguino* from fermented corn. Casa Piedra was still pretty much in the nineteenth century in Vasquez's childhood.

Vasquez says he never encountered prejudice as a child; Anglo and Mexican children attended the same school and played together at Casa Piedra. His transition to the twentieth century started when he moved to Marfa to live with relatives and go to high school. He does not mention encountering prejudice in Marfa, except to say that the barbershops were segregated. His transition was completed when he dropped out of high school in 1943 to join the army and serve with a tank battalion in Europe. After the war Vasquez married and settled down in Marfa, where he opened a garage and auto repair business. While he was in that business he served on the boards of the Chamber of Commerce, the school district, the gas company, and the appraisal district. He retired in 1997. At eighty-six, Armando Vasquez is still an active and highly respected citizen of Marfa.

The Villaba and Vasquez families had very different experiences in the Big Bend, or at least their experiences were remembered differently. I predict that as more of the secret history finds its way into print—and I am sure it will—it will become clear that there is no single "Hispanic experience" in the Big Bend, any more than there is a single Anglo experience. I look forward to the day when the secret history is no longer a secret.

October 13, 2011

✥ 55 ✥

TONY CANO'S MARFA

SEVERAL WEEKS ago I wrote a
column about the Big Bend's
secret history, the story of the Spanish-speaking communities here,
and I mentioned a couple of recent books that threw some light on
the history. Now Tim Johnson of the Marfa Book Company has
called my attention to a third book, Tony Cano's autobiographical
novel, *The Other Side of the Tracks*, published in 2001 by Cano's
own Reata Press in Canutillo, Texas.

Cano grew up poor in Marfa in the 1950s. His father was a fine
cowboy and was a ranch manager on Wayne Cartledge's 9K Ranch
on the Texas-New Mexico line, but he was a heavy drinker. Cano's
mother left him when Cano was in the first grade, moving to
Marfa with her three children and taking a job as a waitress. She
had a difficult time making ends meet. In a recent phone interview, Cano told me that sometimes he and his brother would
come home from school for lunch and there would be nothing in
the house to eat but cornflakes.

Marfa's elementary schools were segregated in the 1950s, and,
like all Mexican American children, Cano went to Blackwell
School. But when he reached the seventh grade he enrolled in
Marfa Elementary, the Anglo-American school whose graduates
went on to Marfa High School. *The Other Side of the Tracks* grew
out of the prejudice that Cano experienced there and at Marfa
High, and out of the ways that he and a small group of friends
decided to fight it. The novel is about the adventures of a group of
Mexican American teenagers who called themselves the
Chinglers, a word derived from a Spanish verb that cannot be

translated in a family newspaper. The book is a frank and unflinching picture of what it was like to be poor and Mexican American in Marfa in the 1950s. It should be required reading for every newcomer to Marfa, because it explains some of the tensions that still underlie the idyllic images of Marfa and its arts community that have recently appeared in national publications.

The Chinglers broke a taboo by secretly dating Anglo-American girls. Fifty years later, Cano still remembers the sting of that particular prejudice. "You couldn't date Anglo girls," he told me. "You couldn't even talk to them in the hallway. We did it because they told us we couldn't." He told me about one Anglo boy who was in love with a Mexican American girl. He and a Mexican American friend had an arrangement by which they would pick up each other's dates, then meet and exchange girls for the evening, meeting again before taking their respective non-dates home. Another unspoken rule was maintaining a racial balance on high school athletic teams; in the novel a coach is fired for playing an all Mexican American basketball team, even though it is a spectacularly winning team. Cano puts his finger on the far-reaching ramifications of high school athletics in a small Texas town; something else that some newcomers to Marfa may have a hard time understanding.

The book is more memoir than novel. The ending is somewhat clumsy, and Cano told me that was the only part that did not really happen; all of the other incidents are factual. He said that he cast it as a novel "for legal reasons." When word got out in Marfa that he was writing a book, several people threatened to sue him if he used their names in it, and that put him on guard.

Cano told me that he wrote the novel "as therapy." Even as an adult, he said, he had a lot of anger about the way Mexican Americans were treated in Texas. "Writing the book took a monkey off my back. I learned to put the past behind me," he said. *The Other Side of the Tracks* is not Cano's only book. He and his wife, poet Ann Sochat, have published a Dutch oven cookbook and a book of poems and ranch reminiscences, *Echoes in the Wind*. Their most recent collaboration was *Bandito*, a biography of Cano's great-grandfather, the revolutionist and bandit Chico Cano. *The Other Side of the Tracks*, however, was a solo effort on Cano's part. He told me that he credits his self-confidence as a writer to two of his Marfa English teachers who saw him as more than a Mexican American troublemaker. "Mrs. Emma Lou Howard taught me how to stand up and talk to a group, and Ms. Mary Lou Kelley made me sit on the front row my senior year and motivated me to do well. If it were not for Ms. Kelley I would not have graduated from high school."

Tony Cano went on from Marfa High to have a career worthy of another book. When he graduated from high school, he told me, his mother gave him $68 and said, "You're a man." He ended up in El Paso, where he got a job working in a Mr. Quick hamburger stand. "When I was twenty-one," he told me, "I said, 'Tony, is this it? Is this what you are going to do the rest of your life?'" He enrolled in Texas Western College, now the University of Texas at El Paso, went on to complete a BA at the University of Missouri, and did graduate work as a teaching assistant at the University of Hawaii.

Cano eventually got into the garment manufacturing business in El Paso and ended up the owner of his own company, Tony Cano Sportswear. Cano's factory became a leading producer of sports jackets for auto-racing teams, a narrow but profitable niche. Cano told me that came about because in 1981 he went to Phoenix to see his first auto race. He was impressed by the skill of the drivers, and after the race he went down to congratulate the winner, Bobby Unser. One thing led to another, and he became a regular weekend volunteer on Unser's pit team, eventually being assigned to holding the pit board, the blackboard that tells the driver how many laps he has to go. He designed a set of jackets for the Unser team, and so many other drivers admired them that the next year eight of the thirty-three teams at the Indianapolis 500 were wearing Tony Cano jackets.

Cano is now retired and travels all over the world with his wife. He says that someday he will write a sequel to *The Other Side of the Tracks*, and it will have a happy ending.

December 1, 2011

✢ 56 ✢

THE SANDIA SPRINGS WETLANDS

IN THE FALL of 2010, Ellen Weinacht of Balmorhea went on a birding trip with some friends to the Bosque del Apache National Wildlife Refuge in New Mexico. As she was watching hundreds of sandhill cranes feeding in the wetlands along the Rio Grande, she thought, "I want a place like this at home." Now she has one. It is called the Sandia Springs Wetlands, and I spent a day last week visiting it with Weinacht and one of the people who helped her create it, David Hedges of Fort Davis.

The Sandia Springs Wetlands is actually a land restoration project. Four hundred years ago Balmorhea was what the Spanish called a *cienega*, a marsh. Antonio de Espejo used that word to describe the area when he camped there in 1583 on his way back home from an expedition to New Mexico. The *cienega* was fed by six springs, now called Phantom Lake, San Solomon, Giffen, Saragosa, and West and East Sandia springs. These springs all rise from a five-hundred-foot-thick layer of Cretaceous limestone that underlies Balmorhea, a layer of rock that is riddled with fissures and caverns that hold water. The largest of the springs, San Solomon, which now empties into the swimming pool at Balmorhea State Park, has historically flowed at about twenty million gallons a day. Phantom Lake spring, several miles west of San Solomon, issues from a cave in a limestone bluff and produces about three million gallons a day. Add in the other four springs, and that's a lot of water. When Espejo arrived he found the Jumano Indians using it to irrigate fields of corn and beans.

In the 1850s, Mexican settlers from Chihuahua arrived and

built irrigation ditches leading from San Solomon spring to their fields. They called their settlement, which clustered around the base of the little ridge that runs just east of present-day Balmorhea, Indio. A large cross on top of the end of that ridge, easily visible from the Carrasco store across the highway, marks the spot today. They probably also gave San Solomon spring its name, which is something of a mystery since there is no San Solomon on the Catholic calendar of saints. The name probably comes from an Indian word that sounded like "San Solomon" to those settlers. In 1896 a post office was established at Indio and the name was changed to Brogado, supposedly in honor of Father Brocadus Ecken, the Dutch Carmelite priest at St. Joseph's Church in Fort Davis who held services in Indio. The name Balmorhea did not appear on the map until 1906, when a town site by that name was platted between Indio and San Solomon spring by three land pro-moters named Balcum, Morrow, and Rhea, thus *Bal-mo-rhea*.

In 1871, Fort Davis entrepreneur and land speculator Daniel Murphy established a farm near San Solomon spring and dug a canal that diverted the water to his vegetable crops, which he sold to the army at Fort Davis. The adjacent landowners objected, and a series of lawsuits that kept the courts busy through most of the 1870s and '80s resulted in a ruling that Murphy had to share the water with his neighbors. Eventually a network of irrigation canals and ditches grew up around all six springs, and by the time Lake Balmorhea was built and the Reeves County Water Improvement District Number One was created in 1915, the marshes had been drained and turned into fields and pastures.

Weinacht and Hedges have taken a small step toward reversing that process. They have created three small ponds, fed by the Sandia Canal, and are building a fourth pond the size of the first three combined. When completed, the wetlands will cover about six acres and will provide a habitat for migrating shorebirds. The ponds are easily accessible to the public from County Road 313, which runs south from State Highway 17, just where the state highway turns west after crossing under Interstate 10. There are three inviting picnic tables beside the ponds.

The morning that Hedges and Weinacht and I were there was sunny and pleasantly cool. There had been a severe hailstorm the previous evening, and shredded leaves from cottonwood trees covered the ground around us. Shorebirds were already arriving. As we sat at one of the picnic tables and talked, a flight of half a dozen or so western sandpipers skimmed over the water and settled on the pond nearest us, immediately standing up in the shallow water and plucking organisms out of it with their long bills. "They are on their way to Alaska, where they nest in the spring," Hedges said. "I'm surprised that they have any feathers left after last night," Weinacht said, adding that eight inches of hail had fallen at Saragosa, just up the road. We also saw several families of northern shoveler ducks on the other side of the pond, and as we walked between the ponds, scared up a green-winged teal that was resting in a clump of grass on the bank. She flew off to join a cinnamon teal and a blue-winged teal paddling on the water. These birds, Hedges pointed out, were just the beginning of the spring migration.

The remarkable thing about the Sandia Springs Wetlands is that Ellen Weinacht and her husband, Don, created it themselves, on their own land, with absolutely no aid from the federal, state, or local government, and they have made it available to the public. When they first got the idea they consulted Hedges and Madge Lindsay of Fort Davis, who are fellow birders and naturalists. Hedges helped them pick the site, using a soil map of Reeves County to locate a patch of clayey soil that would hold water. They have enlisted the Tierra Grande chapter of the Texas Master Naturalists to assist with the planning and development, and the master naturalists have created committees of volunteers to help with water management, interpretation, and plant species. But the project is pure, uncluttered, non-bureaucratic private enterprise, done in the straightforward Texas way. The Weinachts had a good idea and went ahead with it. As the Gary P. Nunn songs says, *When a Texan fancies he'll take his chances, chances will be taken.*

April 26, 2012

✤ 57 ✤

AFTER THE FIRE

I AM HESITANT to write about the fire that swept through Fort Davis the evening of April 9, destroying twenty-four homes, because I was not even there when it hit. My wife and I were returning from a trip to New Mexico that Saturday, and we were stopped at a roadblock in Balmorhea. A state trooper told us that we could not go to Fort Davis because the town had been evacuated and was in flames. We spent Saturday night in a motel in Balmorhea, not knowing whether we would have a house to go home to or not.

I decided in the motel that the best way to deal with the situation was to assume that our house had burned down and we had lost everything. If that proved not to be true, I reasoned, I would be elated, and if it were at least I would be prepared for it. We had our suitcases from our trip in the car with several changes of clothing, our computer, a coffeepot, and a bottle of wine, and that, I thought, would be enough to make a fresh start on. My wife, on the other hand, thought my attitude was nonsense. She was sure our house was undamaged, she said, and she rolled over and went to sleep. I woke up every half hour, trying to remember who held our homeowner's insurance policy, which I keep in a drawer in my desk, trying to figure out how I was going to pay our income tax if our checkbooks were burned up; and remembering family photographs and mementos that I was going to miss.

Curiously, the thing I thought that I would miss the most was a little three-inch-high lead figure of a black man smoking a cigar and wearing white trousers, a short green jacket, and a gray derby hat that my father brought me from a business trip to Richmond, Virginia, when I was four years old. I think he bought it at the magazine stand in the railroad station there. It is the only tangible object I have from my early childhood, and it has stood on my desk for many years. It turned out that my wife was right. Our house and our neighborhood survived the fire and my little lead man is still on my desk.

Two things about the fire are astonishing in retrospect. The first is that no lives were lost in Fort Davis, even though part of town was an inferno that night. The other is the way that people here have helped each other in the days since it struck. As one of my neighbors said, "We may fuss and fight with each other most of the time, but when the chips are down we all pull together."

It started the night of the fire. In spite of the state troopers driving through town telling people to evacuate, some people chose to stay in town and fight the fire. They saved not only their own homes but their neighbors'. Bud and Adele Coffey live just off South Front Street, where several houses burned. Bud told me that he was not home when the order to evacuate came; he and his son Ross had driven down to Mano Prieto to turn a friend's horses out of their pen in order to save them from the approaching flames. When they got back they found Adele packing the car. "We're not leaving," he told her. "We've got to stay here and keep our house from burning down."

"We saw the fire hit Dolores Mountain," Bud told me. "It came down the side of the mountain in about five minutes and hit the McMurrays' old house. The butane tank there exploded, and the flames were headed across the vacant lot towards Kelly Fenstermaker's house. We had our garden hose hooked up and were wetting down our house, and we got another hooked up and wet down that lot, and that saved Kelly's house. The wind was blowing so hard the water was blowing back in our faces, and we had to get real close to the fire to do any good." The Coffeys managed to wet down one more house before the power went out and their pump stopped working. They saved that house with wet gunnysacks. They were by no means the only ones trying to save other people's houses that night.

That same night, Joe and Lanna Duncan opened their El Capitan Hotel in Van Horn free to all Fort Davis evacuees. At their Limpia Hotel here in Fort Davis, the employees left and put a sign on the door that said, "Everything is open. Firemen, just find a place to rest."

The Tuesday morning after the fire, ranchers and cowboys from three counties converged on Fort Davis to round up loose livestock. The Miller boys from Valentine, who had been here Saturday night fighting the fire, showed up. Jon Means came from Van Horn with three cowboys and a stock trailer. There were at least half a dozen other stock trailers in town that day, and twice that many pickups towing trailers with saddled horses. They worked their way up Highway 17, where all the fences had burned, sorting out cattle from at least five ranches and moving them to unburned pastures. Somewhere along the way they acquired a stray Shetland pony. Someone penned seven displaced Shetlands in a fenced yard in Fort Davis that evening.

Then there is the hay. The first truckload of round bales rolled in from Fort Stockton, ninety miles away, just a few days after the fire. They were sent by ranchers there who knew ranchers here. The trucks have kept coming, two or three a day, as word has spread through the ranching community that there are ranchers here without feed. They are now arriving from as far away as Oklahoma and Tucumcari, New Mexico. The trucking charges have been paid by ranchers and 4-H clubs all over the state. The bales are stacked up in Curtis Evans's pasture south of town, and County Agent Logan Boswell is making them available to anyone whose pastures have burned.

For the past two weeks the standard greeting in Fort Davis has been, "Y'all all right? Your house all right?" Those who lost their homes are soldiering on and trying to smile. At Jerry and Jeanne Yarbrough's place, which was a pile of rubble the day after the fire, the lot has been scraped clean. But their flagpole is still standing, and new American and Texas flags are flying from it. That is the West Texas way.

April 28, 2011

Photo by Bill Wright

LONN TAYLOR is a historian and writer who retired to Fort Davis, Texas, with his wife, Dedie, after twenty years as a historian at the Smithsonian Institution's National Museum of American History in Washington, DC. He received a BA in history and government from Texas Christian University in 1961 and did graduate work at New York University before returning to Texas to enter the museum field. He served as curator and director of the University of Texas at Austin's Winedale Historical Center from 1970 to 1977; as curator of history at the Dallas Historical Society from 1977 to 1979; and as curator and deputy director of the Museum of New Mexico in Santa Fe from 1980 to 1984. Taylor's books include *Texas Furniture: The Cabinetmakers and Their Work, 1840-1880* (with David Warren, University of Texas Press, 1975, revised edition, 2012); *The American Cowboy* (with Ingrid Maar, Library of Congress, 1983); *New Mexican Furniture, 1600-1940* (with Dessa Bokides, Museum of New Mexico Press, 1987); *The Star-Spangled Banner: The Flag That Inspired the National Anthem* (Harry N. Abrams, 2000); *The Star-Spangled Banner: The Making of an American Icon* (with Kathlenn Kendrick and Jeffrey Brodie, Smithsonian Books, 2008); and *Texas, My Texas: Musings of the Rambling Boy* (TCU Press, 2012). He writes a weekly column about Texas called "The Rambling Boy," for the Marfa *Big Bend Sentinel*.